Collins

easy learning

Portuguese

in a click

Sofia Carvalho Martins Carlos

HarperCollins Publishers
77-85 Fulham Palace Road
London W6 8JB
Great Britain

www.collinslanguage.com

First edition 2010

Reprint 10 9 8 7 6 5 4 3 2 1 0

© HarperCollins Publishers 2010

ISBN 978-0-00-733737-8

Collins® is a registered trademark of
HarperCollins Publishers Limited

A catalogue record for this book is available
from the British Library

Typeset by Q2AMedia

Audio material recorded and produced by
Networks SRL, Milan

Printed and Bound in China by Leo Paper
Products Ltd.

Editorial Director: Eva Martinez

Series Editor: Rob Scriven

Contents

Introduction

Welcome to *Collins Easy Learning Portuguese in a Click*. This is a new course which aims to give you all the skills you'll need to start understanding and using Portuguese quickly, easily and effectively in real situations.

This course is aimed at adult learners with no previous experience of Portuguese. We've thought about which situations would be most useful to you during a visit to Portugal, and have created a course that embraces all the main scenarios a traveller would be likely to encounter, such as public transport, checking into a hotel, shopping, eating out, visiting a museum and going to a football match.

Our approach is not to bombard you with too much grammar, but rather to let you listen to authentic dialogues set in useful situations, giving you the nuts and bolts of what's being said, then guiding you through carefully gauged practice exercises to increase your confidence.

The tools you need to succeed

The course has been designed to provide you with three essential tools in order to make your language learning experience a success. In your pack you'll find an activation code for the **online course**, this handy **book**, and an **audio CD**. You can use a combination of these whenever and wherever you are, making the course work for you.

The online course

www.collinslanguage.com/click provides you with a 12-unit online interactive language experience. Listen to a dialogue (and follow the words on-screen if you like) then study the new words and phrases before tackling some fun interactive games and exercises. You'll then also have the chance to perfect your pronunciation by recording your own voice (microphone not provided).

To access the online course simply go to www.collinslanguage.com/click and enter your personal activation code which you will find inside the front cover of this book.

The book

There will be times when it's not practical for you to be at a computer. There will also be times when you simply don't want to stare at the screen. For these times, this pocket-sized book contains the whole course for you in a handy portable format, so you can continue learning without the need for a computer. All of the content you need to learn Portuguese is right here in this book. Study the language and complete the exercises just as you would online.

When you want to check your answers, go to **www.collinslanguage.com/click** to download the answer key.

The audio CD

Use the audio CD to hear native Portuguese speakers engaging in dialogues set in real life situations and use it alongside the book in order to improve your listening comprehension skills. The audio CD can be downloaded to your mp3 player so that you can keep on learning even when you're on the move.

See the website at **www.collinslanguage.com/click** for the written transcript of all the spoken dialogues.

How it works

Portuguese in a Click is divided into 12 units with revision sections after Unit 6 and Unit 12. Each unit begins with a **Traveller's tip**, a short passage highlighting an area of Portuguese life and culture, offering you tips on what to expect when you visit the country.

Following a brief summary of the language structures you're about to study, we move straight on to the first dialogue, headed **Listen up**. Any tricky or useful vocabulary is then explained in the **Words and phrases** box (with accompanying audio online), then we go into a little more detail in **Unlocking the language**. Then it's over to you.

Your Turn offers further practice of each structure and area of vocabulary encountered.

Halfway through each unit, you'll see that the cycle begins again with a fresh **Listen up**. This adds a different dimension to the material and scenario you've already looked at, and provides you with a new challenge in a slightly different situation.

Each unit ends with **Let's Recap**, in which you can check over the language you've used in the unit. The online version then gives you the chance to **record yourself** saying some of the most important vocabulary from the unit, to compare your pronunciation with that of a native speaker.

Collins Easy Learning Portuguese in a Click aims to be fun, but at the same time to equip you with genuinely useful linguistic and cultural tools to make the most of your time in Portugal. We hope you enjoy it!

Muito prazer
Pleased to meet you

We'll look at greetings and how to introduce yourself and say where you're from. You'll also learn how to say where you're going on holiday, and for how long.

Traveller's tip

The boom in affordable package holidays in the 1960s and 70s put Portugal firmly on the map for foreign visitors, and its popularity continues to this day.

Recently, though, many people have started to travel to Portugal independently, whether it be on a short city break, a whistle-stop tour of the major cities, or a fly-drive arrangement allowing them to spend a couple of weeks exploring the World Heritage Torre de Belém in Lisboa, the 13th-century university in Coimbra in the west, the medieval district of Porto in the north, picturesque fishing villages in the Algarve in the south or relaxing on one of the sandy beaches making up 528 miles of the coastline.

The rise of budget airlines, together with the drop in fares charged by long-distance operators, has made Portugal much more accessible to the independent traveller. Internal flights, trains, car hire and accommodation can be booked online, and the increased availability of rural properties to rent by the day, week or month has opened up areas of the country previously unknown to the overseas tourist. You can find more details about this type of trip by searching for **ecoturismo, agroturismo** or **turismo rural** on the internet.

Whatever type of visit to Portugal you're planning, you'll quickly discover the truth of the old tourist-industry slogan **Portugal: país à beira mar plantado e país de contrastes** – Portugal, a country planted by the sea and a country of contrasts.

sete   7

In this unit we'll be working with two useful structures, that allow us to introduce ourselves and to say where we're going.

Sou ...   I am ...
Vou a/para ...   I'm going to ...

Listen up 1

A British woman meets a Portuguese man just before they catch a flight to Faro. Listen to their conversation. You can follow the conversation below as you listen, then you'll find a series of explanations and exercises linked to it on the next few pages.

⊙ 1

Nuno	Olá!
Lyn	Olá, bom dia.
Nuno	Vai para Faro?
Lyn	Sim, vou para Faro.
Nuno	Ah, eu também! Sou o Nuno.
Lyn	Muito prazer. Sou a Lyn.
Nuno	É inglesa?
Lyn	Não, sou escocesa. Sou de Glasgow.
Nuno	Ah, você é de Glasgow.
Lyn	E você é de Faro?
Nuno	Não, sou de Viseu, mas trabalho em Faro. Você é estudante?
Lyn	Sim, sou estudante de Português e Francês.
Nuno	Vai a Faro para praticar Português?
Lyn	Sim, num curso de Verão.
Nuno	Muito bem! Bem, vou até ao café.
Lyn	Está bem. Até logo.
Nuno	Até logo.

Greetings and other useful words

olá, bom dia	hello, good morning
sim/não	yes/no
eu também	so am I/me too
muito prazer	pleased to meet you
mas	but
num curso *m* de Verão *m*	on a summer course
muito bem	fine/very well
bem ...	well ...
está bem	OK (literally: it's all right)
até logo	see you later

Verbs

(Você) Vai a/para ...?	Are you going to ...?
Vou a/para ...	I'm going to ...
Sou de ...	I am from
Você é ...?	Are you ...?
trabalho	I work
praticar	to practise

Some nationalities

inglês/inglesa	English *m/f*
escocês/escocesa	Scottish *m/f*
português/portuguesa	Portuguese *m/f*
francês/francesa	French *m/f*

A few occupations

estudante	student
professor/professora	teacher *m/f*
artista	artist

In this section we explain some of the words and expressions introduced in the dialogue.

o português/**a** portuguesa	'the Portuguese man/woman'. All nouns in Portuguese are either masculine or feminine. Masculine nouns use **o** to mean 'the' while feminine nouns use **a**.
Você é inglesa/de Faro/ estudante?	'**Are you** English *f*/from Faro/a student?'
Sou escocesa/de Viseu/ estudante.	'**I'm** Scottish/from Viseu/a student.' **Sou** ('I am') and **é** ('he/she is') are both parts of the verb **ser** ('to be'). **É** can also mean 'it is' (**é interessante**).
	You can also see that 'I'm a student' is just **sou estudante**. You don't say 'a' before a job or occupation in Portuguese.
inglês/inglesa *m/f* português/portuguesa *m/f*	Notice that nationalities are spelt with a small letter, and that their endings vary depending on whether the person is male or female.
Você vai para Faro? **Vou** para Faro.	'**Are you going** to Faro?' '**I'm going** to Faro.' **Vou** ('I'm going') and **vai** ('you're going') are parts of the verb **ir** ('to go').

Look again at the dialogue (Listen up 1). Are the following statements true or false? You will find the answers to all of the exercises in this book online at www.collinslanguage.com/click 1

1. They are travelling to Porto. ....

2. Lyn is English. ....

3. Nuno works in Faro. ....

Check your understanding of the dialogue by answering these questions. 1

1. What does Lyn study? ....

2. Where is Nuno going at the end of the conversation? ....

Find expressions in the dialogue (track 1) to convey the following:

1. Good morning
2. Pleased to meet you
3. Me too
4. Are you going to Faro?
5. Yes, I'm going to Faro.
6. Are you a student?
7. Yes, I'm a student of Portuguese and French.
8. See you later.

> ## Pronunciation Tip
>
> Portuguese pronunciation is generally straightforward, with each letter pronounced logically.
>
> **Sou português**
>
> In Portuguese the letter **s** is pronounced as 'sh' at the end of a word ('portuguê**s'**) or when it precedes a consonant ('e**s**tudante').

- -

Ask a female the following questions. Check your answers by listening to the audio track.

1. Are you French?
2. Are you English?

- -

Say the following in Portuguese. Check your answers by listening to the audio track.

1. I am Portuguese. (*Try both male and female*)
2. I am from Faro.
3. I am a student.

- -

Listen to track 3 and then answer these questions:

1. Where is João from? ....
2. What is his occupation? ....
3. What is Ana's nationality? ....
4. What is her job? ....

Match the Portuguese expressions on the left with their meanings on the right:

1. Sou australiano/australiana.
2. Trabalho num escritório.
3. Vou até ao café.
4. Sou estudante de italiano.
5. Você é irlandês/irlandesa?
6. É muito interessante.

Are you Irish?
It's very interesting.
I'm studying Italian.
I'm Australian.
I'm going to the café.
I work in an office.

 ## Listen up 2

Listen to Pedro and Teresa talking about themselves – their work and their studies. ⊙ 4

Pedro	Olá, boa tarde. Sou o Pedro. Sou português, de Évora, mas vivo e trabalho em Lisboa. Sou professor de Matemática. Também sou estudante de fotografia. Agora vou a uma aula de fotografia. Logo vou jantar a um restaurante com os meus colegas de turma.
Teresa	Olá, sou a Teresa. Sou portuguesa, de Aveiro, mas vivo no Porto. Não trabalho. Sou estudante de História. Agora vou a uma aula. Logo vou a um bar com o meu namorado.

boa tarde	good afternoon/evening
vivo	I live
professor(a) de Matemática	Maths teacher
fotografia *f*	photography
aula *f*	class
agora	now
logo	later on/then
jantar a um restaurante	to have dinner in a restaurant
com meus colegas	with my colleagues/classmates
turma *f*	group (in a school)
não trabalho	I don't work
História *f*	History
bar *m*	bar
namorado/namorada	boyfriend/girlfriend

🔓 Unlocking the language 2

viv**o** e trabalh**o**	'I live and (I) work'. Most verbs saying what I do ('I study', 'I travel', etc.) end in **-o** in Portuguese. Unfortunately, both **sou** and **vou** are exceptions!
um bar/**uma** aula	Notice that the word for 'a' can be **um** or **uma**. This depends on whether the noun it goes with is considered masculine (**um bar**) or feminine (**uma aula**). **Um/uma** can also mean 'one' – see below.

Numbers 1–12

1	**um** (when it stands alone) **um** bar – working with a masculine noun (*singular*) **uma** aula – working with a feminine noun (*singular*)
2	**dois** (when it stands alone) **dois** professores – working with the masculine noun (*plural*) **duas** aulas – working with the feminine noun (*plural*)
3, 4, 5, 6, 7	**três, quatro, cinco, seis, sete**
8, 9, 10, 11, 12	**oito, nove, dez, onze, doze**

Below is the transcript from Listen Up 2 but lots of words have been missed out. Use the vocabulary that you have learned so far, fill in the gaps:

⊙ 4

Olá, boa tarde. .... o Pedro. Sou ...., de Évora, mas

vivo e trabalho em .... Sou professor de Matemática. Também sou

.... de fotografia. Agora .... a uma aula de fotografia.

Logo .... jantar a um restaurante com os meus colegas de

....

.... , sou a Teresa. Sou ...., de Aveiro, mas vivo no

.... Não trabalho. .... estudante de História. Agora

.... a uma aula. Logo .... a um bar com o meu

namorado.

••

Rewrite the following to create Portuguese numbers:

ITOO	ROTQAU	SÊRT	VONE	ZONE
....	....	....	....	....
ZDE	EISS	AUM	IODS	NICCO
....	....	....	....	....
MU	TESE	AUSD	ZODE	
....	....	....	....	

••

Say the following in Portuguese. Check your answers by listening to the audio track.

⊙ 5

1. Hello.
2. I am English. *(try both male and female)*
3. I live in Lisboa.
4. I am a student.

Listen and understand. In which order are the numbers 1–12 ⊙ 6
pronounced? Mark the order against the list of Portuguese
numbers below:

um	cinco	nove
dois	seis	dez
três	sete	onze
quatro	oito	doze

....

There are two mistakes in the following text. Can you spot them?

Olá, bom dia. Sou a Maria. Sou português. Vivo em Sintra, mas sou Santarém. Sou
economista.

⟳ Let's recap

Here's an opportunity for you to revise the language you've learned in this
unit. Supply the correct option in each case:

1. Você .... portuguesa?

   a. sou   b. vou   c. é

2. Não, não .... portuguesa.

   a. vou   b. sou   c. vai

3. Você .... a Faro?

   a. vou   b. é   c. vai

4. Sim, ... a Faro.

   a. é   b. vou   c. sou

....

Write the numbers 1–12 in Portuguese. We've started you off:

1. um	7.	
2. dois	8.	
3.	9.	
4.	10.	
5.	11.	
6.	12.	

Onde é ...?
Where is ...?

2

You'll learn how to find your way around using public transport, and to locate places you need to find. We'll also study how to say at what time things happen.

Traveller's tip

Public transport in Portugal is excellent value for money. Local bus services – and, in some of the larger cities, tram and **metro** (underground train) networks – have benefited from huge investment and visitors are often surprised at how cheap transport is when compared to their home countries.

One of the main advantages of the bus system in Portuguese cities is that there is generally one (very reasonable) fixed fare, however many stops you wish to travel. A single ticket will sometimes allow you to combine travel on a bus and a metro train to reach your destination. Further savings can be made by buying a multi-journey ticket – **um bilhete multiviagem** – giving you, say, ten journeys for the price of eight.

Carristur was founded in **Lisboa** in 1982 to develop tourism in the city. The company now offers a wide range of tours in the Lisbon area, and the tour maps can be found

online. There is even a free bus which goes from **Belém** to **Marquês de Pombal** and back again on Fridays, Saturdays and the days before each Bank Holiday.

Travelling between cities by **comboio** (train) is a delight in modern, clean, comfortable trains which are also remarkably affordable. The national rail network, **CP**, has a number of inter-city jewels in its crown, notably the high-speed **Alfa Pendular** between **Lisboa** and **Porto**. The network also has **Regional** trains, which stop at every station, and **Inter-regional** trains, which stop at selected stations.

TAP Portugal offers an affordable shuttle service known as the **ponte aérea** – literally 'air bridge' – between **Lisboa** and **Porto**.

In the last unit we met a verb **ser** ('to be') which we used to say things about ourselves. We can use either **ser** or a new verb **ficar** to say where things are located. We'll also learn the language you need to say at what time a bus or train leaves and arrives.

A que horas ...?   At what time ...?
Onde é ...?/Onde fica ...?   Where is ...?

 ## Listen up 1

We've arrived in Portugal and are outside the airport looking to ⊙ 7
continue the journey to our destination. Listen to the sequence of
short dialogues as many times as you need to. First we need to ask
where the bus stop is:

Tourist	Olá.
Passer-by	Bom dia.
Tourist	Onde é a paragem de autocarros?
Passer-by	É ali, à direita.
Tourist	Ah, sim. Obrigado.
Passer-by	De nada.

Now we're in the city centre looking for the underground station. ⊙ 8
Another passer-by is telling us that it's in the main street:

Tourist	Por favor, onde é a estação de metro?
Passer-by	É na rua principal.
Tourist	Muito obrigada. •
Passer-by	De nada.

Now we need to buy a ticket – just a one-way ticket for now. You'll ⊙ 9
hear the expression for "one-way ticket" as well as the price:

Tourist	Um bilhete de ida, por favor.
Clerk	São dois euros.
Tourist	Obrigado.

We're going on a day trip to the historic town of Sintra, but this time we need a return ticket. Listen carefully and try to catch the price: 10

Tourist	Quero ir para Sintra, ida e volta. Quanto é?
Clerk	São doze euros, por favor.
Tourist	Muito obrigada. Muito boa tarde.
Clerk	De nada. Boa tarde.

🔊 Words and phrases 1

Onde é/fica ...?	Where is ...?
É/Fica ...	It's ...
a paragem de autocarros	the bus stop
ali/aqui	there/here
à direita	on the right
à esquerda	on the left
(muito) obrigada *f*/obrigado *m*	thank you (very much). Women always use **obrigada** while men always use **obrigado**.
de nada	you're welcome/not at all
por favor	please/excuse me
são	it is (lit. 'they are')
a estação de metro	the underground station
a rua principal	the main street
um bilhete de ida	a single ticket
(um bilhete de) ida e volta	(a) return (ticket)
Quero ir para ...	I want to go to ...
Quanto é?	How much is (it)?
Muito boa tarde	(A very) good afternoon

Unlocking the language 1

So far we have learned one way of saying 'to be' in Portuguese:

Onde **é** a paragem de autocarros?   Where's the bus stop?

É ali.   It's there.

Ser is used for many purposes: we've already seen **sou o João, sou português, sou de Lisboa, sou economista,** and now we can add prices to this list:

Quanto **é** (o bilhete)?   How much is it (/is the ticket)?

É um euro/**são** dois euros.   It's one euro/two euros.

Notice that for something costing two euros upwards, the seller will say **são** (literally 'they are', rather than 'it is').

You'll have noticed the accent on the words **é** and **até**. The rules for why a word has an accent are quite complicated, but a useful guide is that you should pronounce any vowel with an accent on it more heavily than other vowels in the word: e.g. **EH** (as in 'get') and a-**TEH**.

 ## Your turn 1

Listen again to tracks 9 and 10. Are the following statements true  9-10 **or false? Remember you can check your answers online at www. collinslanguage.com/click.**

1. The single ticket was 3 euros.   2.   The return to Sintra was 12 euros.

• •

Match the photos with the Portuguese word for each form of transport. there is one you don't know yet but you should be able to work it out by a process of elimination:

1. o autocarro

2. o metro

3. o táxi

4. o comboio

a.

b.

c.

d.

Find expressions in the dialogues to convey the following: 7–10

1. Where is the bus stop? ....

2. Where is the metro station? ....

3. How much is it? ....

4. It's ten euros. ....

Make sure you can also say the following:

1. hello

2. please

3. thanks

4. many thanks

5. not at all

6. goodbye

Pronunciation Tip

um bilhete de ida
You pronounce the Portuguese *lh* similarly to 'lli' in the English 'million'.

bilhete   bil-YEH-te

Now try another phrase you already know:

não trabalho ...   I don't work ...

Ask for the following tickets in Portuguese. You can check your answers by listening to the audio track.   11

1. To Lisboa, return, please.

2. A single ticket.

Now try to remember how to ask these two questions. Again, listen to the audio track to check your answers.   11 2

1. Where is the bus stop?

2. How much is it?

Listen to the conversation on track 13 and answer the questions: ◎ 13

1. Where does the lady want to go? ....
2. What sort of ticket does she ask for? ....
3. How much does it cost? ....

. . . .

Rearrange the word order in these expressions so that they make sense:

1. favor de ida por um bilhete ....
2. estação é onde a? ....
3. euros dez são ....
4. principal na rua está ....

Listen up 2

Now we are at the bus station. The passenger wants to get a bus to the capital. We're told what time it leaves and what time it arrives. ◎ 14

Passenger	A que horas parte o autocarro?
Clerk	Parte às quatro e meia.
Passenger	E a que horas chega a Lisboa?
Clerk	Chega aproximadamente às seis menos um quarto.
Passenger	Muito obrigada.

Making enquiries at the railway station. The customer wants to go to the university town of Coimbra. ◎ 15

Passenger	Boa tarde.
Clerk	Olá, boa tarde.
Passenger	A que horas parte o comboio para Coimbra?
Clerk	Parte às dez.
Passenger	E a que horas chega a Coimbra?
Clerk	Chega a Coimbra às onze e cinco.
Passenger	Quanto é?
Clerk	São seis euros só de ida e onze para ida e volta.
Passenger	Muito bem. Obrigado.
Clerk	De nada.

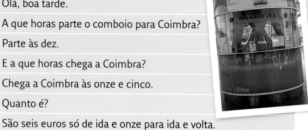

Adeus	Goodbye
A que horas parte?	At what time does it leave?
parte	it leaves/departs
autocarro	bus
comboio *m*	train
aproximadamente	approximately
A que horas chega?	At what time does it arrive?
chega	it arrives
só de ida	just one way

Unlocking the language 2

Telling the time

In Portugal the 24-hour clock is used to tell the time. This means the day runs
from midnight to midnight and is divided into 24 hours, numbered from 0 to 23
(1–12 equals am and 12–24 equals pm). However, when people read the time, they
mostly use 1–12 (e.g. O comboio parte às 16.00. – read 'às quatro').

A que horas?   The basic question really asks 'at what hour?' Then
                      you can add a verb ...

A que horas **chega**?   At what time **does it arrive?**

Chega às onze.   **It arrives** at eleven o'clock.

Notice that the verb is the same in the question and the answer.

'At' a particular time:

à uma   at one o'clock

às duas   at two o'clock

às três   at three o'clock

Notice that the **à** at 1.00 becomes **às** for times from 2.00 to 12.00. It becomes **ao**
for **ao meio-dia** ('at noon').

Here's how to say some more complex times:

at 11.05	às onze e cinco
at 11.10	às onze e dez
at 11.15	às onze e **um quarto**
at 11.30	às onze e **meia**
at 11.45	às **doze** menos um quarto *or* a um quarto para o meio-dia (lit: a quarter to noon)
at 11.50	às **doze** menos dez *or* ao **meio-dia** menos dez *or* às **onze** e cinquenta
at 11.55	às **doze** menos cinco *or* ao **meio-dia** menos cinco *or* às **onze** e cinquenta e cinco

So **e** matches the 'past' half of the English clock, and **menos** equates to minutes 'to' the next hour.

 ## Your turn 2

Match up the clock faces with the times shown beneath:

1. cinco e um quarto
2. sete menos um quarto
3. onze e dez
4. nove

a.   b.

c.   d.

Write the following in full in Portuguese:

1. at 16.10
2. at 18.15
3. at 9.30
4. at 10.45
5. at 12.55 (*be careful!*)

Pronunciation Tip

às nove e meia

The **e** meaning 'and' is pronounced *ee* as in 'eat' (as opposed to the **é** with an accent from the previous unit meaning 'he/she/it is' which is pronounced *eh* as in 'get'.)

Can you say the following in Portuguese?

1. The train leaves at three o'clock.   2. The bus arrives at ten o'clock.

....

Listen to the dialogue on track 17 and answer these questions: ◉ 17

1. Where is the passenger going? ....

2. What time does the train leave? ....

3. What time does it get to its destination? ....

....

Answer the following questions in Portuguese, using the prompts in brackets:

1. Onde é a estação de metro? (*main street*) ....

2. Quanto é um bilhete de ida? (*4 euros*) ....

3. A que horas parte o comboio? (*9.15*) ....

4. A que horas chega o autocarro? (*9.50*) ....

Let's recap

Here's an opportunity for you to revise the language you've learned in this unit.

Use one of the following words to fill each of the gaps below:

parte	ali	o	chega	a	é
horas	Quanto	quarto	bilhete	Onde	

1. .... a paragem de autocarros?

2. .... que horas .... o comboio para Lisboa?

3. Sai às duas menos um ....

4. A que horas .... a Lisboa?

5. A que .... sai .... autocarro?

6. .... é um .... de ida e volta?

7. É ...., à direita.

Uma ajuda
A bit of help

We'll put together an essential survival kit, to cover any situations in which you might run into problems, from simply not understanding to more complex situations involving injury, loss of possessions and the like.

⋯Traveller's tip⋯

Among the problems expressed by students of Portuguese are the notions that the Portuguese talk much more quickly, and make more nasal sounds than speakers of English, and that regional accents can be hard to follow. The speed issue may or may not be true, but it's inevitable that there will be times when you don't catch what's been said to you, so we're going to focus on a few expressions to make it clear that you haven't understood, to ask for things to be repeated, and so on.

It's fair to say that Portugal is generally a safe, friendly and easy-going country in which to spend time, but in any city or country there will always be a minority element looking to pick your pocket or trick you in some way. Such people are found especially in Lisboa and in particular during the city's Festivals of Saints. We'll show you what you need to say if you've lost your passport or your money etc. Of course, if you see something that makes you suspicious, call the police or ask for directions to the nearest police station.

Equally, you can't never tell when illness might strike, whether at home or abroad. Medical care is free in Portugal and you can expect to receive treatment at a hospital even if you have no proof of identity with you (although it is advisable always to carry your European Health Insurance Card). Doctors and health-service workers are devoted to helping people and no patients are sent away without having been seen by a doctor, no matter what their social or economic circumstances are. We'll equip you with the basic language necessary to explain what's happened so that you can get the correct treatment.

vinte e sete   27

In this unit, as well as focusing on situation-specific language, we'll dip briefly into the past tense to say what has happened. This is a one-off – the rest of the course uses primarily present-tense language.

Perdi o meu passaporte.	I've lost my passport.
Roubaram-me a carteira.	I've had my wallet stolen.
Roubaram-me o passaporte.	I've had my passport stolen.

We'll also have a look at the verb **poder** ('to be able') to ask questions like 'Can you help me?'

Pode-me ajudar?   Can you help me?

Listen up 1

Listen to the series of short expressions on tracks 18 and 19 covering problems of understanding and giving you phrases to use if you get lost. You will have the opportunity to practise them shortly.

⊙ 18-19

From now on you will not see the dialogue written here in the book but you can always go online to access all of the transcripts at www.collinslanguage.com/click.

Words and phrases 1

Como?	Pardon? (not having heard)
Pode repetir, por favor?	Can you repeat, please?
Pode falar mais devagar, por favor?	Can you speak more slowly, please?
Não entendo.	I don't understand.
Não falo Português.	I don't speak Portuguese.
Fala Inglês?	Do you speak English?
Sou estrangeiro/a.	I'm a foreigner.
Não sou de cá.	I'm not from here.
Pode-me escrever, por favor?	Will you write it down for me, please?

Desculpe.	Sorry (excuse me). **Com licença** (lit: with permission) is a slightly more formal way of excusing yourself.
Pode-me ajudar?	Can you help me?
Estou perdido/a.	I'm lost.
Onde é a praça principal?	Where's the main square?
Onde é o Hotel Central?	Where's the Hotel Central?
Para a estação de comboios, por favor?	Which way to the railway station, please?
Pode-me por favor mostrar no mapa onde estou?	Can you show me on the map where I am?

Unlocking the language 1

Não entendo/não falo Português/não sou de cá.	Notice that in order to make any verb negative, you just put **não** before it.
Pode-me ajudar? Pode repetir?	**Pode** ('you can' or 'can you?') is part of the verb **poder** ('to be able') and is very useful for asking if someone **can** do something. For the verb that follows it, like 'help' or 'repeat', just use the infinitive form as you find it in the dictionary – you don't need to do any work to it!
Desculpe.	This expression can be used both for attracting attention and for apologising: **Desculpa** (informal)/**desculpe** (polite). The expression **peço desculpa** is used purely for apologising.
Para a ...? Onde é ...?	These structures will be covered in more detail in later units. For the moment, let's just focus on their usefulness in a given situation.

Spend a few minutes looking over Words and phrases 1, then see if you can remember expressions to convey the following:

1. I don't understand

2. Can you repeat, please?

3. more slowly, please

4. I'm not from here

5. Will you write it down for me, please?

6. Can you help me?

The Portuguese alphabet

◎ 20

a	(ah)	**m**	(emm-eh)
b	(beh)	**n**	(enn-eh)
c	(seh, *like 'c' in English 'trace'*)	**o**	(oh)
d	(deh, *like 'dea' in English 'deaf'*)	**p**	(peh)
e	(eh, *as in English 'shed'*)	**q**	(keh)
f	(efe, *like the first four letters of English 'effect'*)	**r**	(er-re, *a bit like the English 'air raid'*)
g	(ge *like 'g' in English 'guess'*)	**s**	(ess-eh)
h	(a-gá)	**t**	(teh)
i	(ee, *like the beginning of the English 'even'*)	**u**	(oo, *as in 'hoover'*)
j	(zho-tah, *like the 's' in English 'leisure'*)	**v**	(veh, *like the English 'v'*)
k	(kappa)	**w**	(dábliu)
l	(ell-eh)	**x**	(sheesh)
		y	(ípsilon, *literally 'Greek letter i'*)
		z	(zeh, *like the English 'z'*)

In addition, the following letter combinations are used quite frequently:
ch, lh, nh, rr

It would be useful at this point to study carefully the letters needed to spell your name and the street and town where you live. Practise spelling these out until you can do it without looking at the guide.

Pronunciation Tip

Pode-me ajudar.
Pode-me ajudar?

As we mentioned earlier on, there's no difference in the written form of a statement and a question, except for the question mark. However, in the spoken form, the question will tend to raise its pitch at the end, just as it would in English. Try saying the expression on the left a few times, first as a statement ('You can help me') then as a question ('Can you help me?')

Your turn 2

How would you say the following in Portuguese? ⊙ 21

1. I'm lost (*spoken by a man*)
2. I'm lost (*spoken by a woman*)
3. I'm foreign (*spoken by a man*)
4. I'm foreign (*spoken by a woman*)

Listen to the people talking, and make sure you have understood ⊙ 22
the problems they're describing.

1. Where does the man want to go? ....
2. Where is the woman from? ....

Match the predicaments on the left with the English translations on the right:

1. Para ...?	I want to go to ...
2. Quero ir para ...	I'm lost.
3. Não entendo.	I don't speak Portuguese.
4. Estou perdido/a.	To get to ...?
5. Não falo Português.	I don't understand.

Listen up 2

Na esquadra da polícia/At the police station ◉ 23

Listen to the dialogue between a tourist and a policeman. The explanatory sections will help you with any words you can't pick out first time.

No hospital (Nas urgências)/At the hospital (A & E) ◉ 24

Now listen to a tourist explaining his problem at the A & E reception desk.

Remember, you can access all of the transcripts online by visiting www.collinslanguage.com/click.

Words and phrases 2

O que é que aconteceu?	What's the problem? (lit: 'What has happened?')
Roubaram-me a carteira.	I've had my wallet stolen.
Não viu nada?	You didn't see anything?
Perdi ...	I've lost ...
dinheiro *m*	money
chaves *f pl*	keys
ligar	to ring
consulado *m*	consulate
Não tem de quê.	Not at all – an alternative to **de nada**
Preencha este formulário.	Fill out this form.
nome *m* completo	first name + surname
endereço *m*	home address
nacionalidade *f*	nationality
contacto *m*	contact (eg. mobile phone, hotel phone number)
Tenho um problema	I have a problem
Tenho o braço inchado.	My arm is swollen (lit: 'I have the arm swollen').

Dói-lhe?/Dói-me muito.	Does it hurt (you)?/It hurts (me) a lot.
chamar	to call
médico *m/f*	doctor
Qual é o seu nome?	What is your name?
estar de férias	to be on holiday
cartão *m* de seguro médico	Health insurance card – if you are an EU citizen, get hold of a European Health Insurance Card before you travel to Portugal: it entitles you to the same treatment as residents in all EU countries.
Sente-se um momento.	Sit down for a moment.

🔒 Unlocking the language 2

One of the potentially confusing things about Portuguese is that there are two ways of saying 'to be'. In the first two units we learned about **ser**, which is used for many purposes. We've seen **sou o Nuno, sou português, sou de Lisboa** and **sou economista,** and we've seen it when talking about prices: **Quanto é? São doze euros**. When we asked where something is located, we used **ser** and we were referring to a permanent location: **Onde é a estação de metro? Onde é o hotel?**

The other verb, **estar**, which also means 'to be' is used to talk about a location/situation of somebody/something, but only about a temporary one (opposed to a permanent location with **ser**):

Pode-me mostrar no mapa onde estou?	Can you show me on the map where I am? (at this moment)
estar de férias	to be on holidays (it doesn't last forever!)
Roubaram-me ...	I've had my ... stolen. Don't worry about the complicated structure: just learn **roubaram-me** (+ **a/as/o/os** + name of item) as a one-off.
Perdi	This is another past tense – again, just focus on the meaning rather than how it's formed. You can start your explanation with **perdi a/as/o/os ....** then list any items lost.
a minha/o meu	**A minha** and **o meu** both mean 'my'. **A minha** is used when the word you are describing is feminine and **o meu** is used when the word is masculine. Two examples you will be familiar with from this unit are **a minha carteira** and **o meu passaporte**. Look out for further examples of this as you continue through the course.

Dói-lhe (o braço)? Dói-me (o braço).	**Dói** comes from **doer** ('to hurt'). What is being said here is 'Does it (your arm) hurt you?'/'It (my arm) hurts me'. If it's needed, the painful body part comes after the **dói-me/-lhe** in both question and statement. Later in the unit you'll learn more names of body parts that could take you to a doctor/hospital.
Diga.	Literally 'tell me' – this is used to invite someone to say what they want to say.

↗ Your turn 3

Match the photos with the Portuguese words to the left:

1. as chaves
2. o dinheiro
3. o cartão de crédito
4. o telemóvel
5. o passaporte
6. a carteira

a.   b.   c.

d.   e.   f.

. . . .

Find expressions in the dialogues to convey the following: ◎ 23–24

1. Can you help me, please? ....
2. I've had my wallet stolen. ....
3. I've lost my passport. ....
4. My arm is swollen. ....
5. It hurts. ....

. . . .

Can you say the following in Portuguese? The language that you ◎ 25
know from the dialogue has been rearranged slightly. Check your
answers by listening to the audio track.

1. I've had my passport stolen.
2. I've lost my wallet.
3. This morning at ten o'clock.

Listen to these two people telling you what has happened to them and then answer the questions:

1. What has been lost in the first instance?
2. What's the problem in the second situation?

Let's recap

In this unit we've set out a couple of usages of a past tense. There's no need to learn the tense, but the expressions themselves are handy to keep in mind. Here's a reminder:

Roubaram-me a/as/o/os   I've had my ... stolen

Perdi ...   I've lost ...

• •

The following sentences have their words in the wrong order. Can you rectify them?

1. favor ajudar pode-me por? ....
2. onde mostrar pode-me no estou mapa? ....
3. carteira roubaram-me a ....
4. braço dói-me o muito ....

• •

Choose the correct option to complete each sentence:

1. Dê-me o .... passaporte, por favor.

   a. de   b. a   c. seu   d. uma

2. Onde .... o Hotel Central?

   a. é   b. sou   c. estou   d. estão

3. Preencha .... formulário, por favor.

   a. esta   b. este   c. estas   d. estes

4. ....-lhe muito?

   a. braço   b. dói   c. tem   d. problema

No hotel
At the hotel

We'll cover the language you'll need to check into a hotel in Portugal and discover what facilities it has to offer. We'll also be taking a look at some of the different types of places to stay in Portugal.

Traveller's tip

Every year, millions of us head to Portugal seeking sunshine, good food and drink, culture and relaxation.

Most hotel and tourism staff speak some English. However, there's a real achievement in speaking some Portuguese on holiday, and the Portuguese will be delighted you've made an effort to learn their language.

Our first experience of a Portuguese hotel is usually on the coasts and in particular in the Algarve as part of a package holiday. But next time, you may want to do things more independently. Here are some of the key words in considering accommodation.

If you are on a budget, **uma pensão** could be for you – modest establishments, often family-run, sometimes with breakfast and private bathroom, but generally without. Facilities are basic, and credit cards are often not accepted.

Backpackers should look out for **uma pousada (de juventude)**, a

(youth) hostel.

Um hotel is indeed a hotel. Expect a higher level of service (and price!), usually with en suite facilities, air-conditioning, etc. Credit cards are widely accepted, and most Portuguese hotels take bookings online.

For an atmospheric, historical setting, try **uma pousada**. These are invariably converted monasteries, convents, castles, stately homes or former municipal buildings turned into hotels, luxuriously appointed but surprisingly affordable, usually between 50 and 100 euros per night. Check out www.pousadas.pt or search on the internet using a term such as **pousadas de Portugal**. Some of the most beautiful pousadas are the one in **Luso-Buçaco** and the Pousada de Portugal in Cascais.

In this unit, we'll mainly be revising two structures we met earlier. They're both very useful for finding your way around and planning your time.

Onde são ...?	Where are ...? (Notice that this time, we're asking about plural things.)
A que horas é ...?	At what time is ...?

 Listen up 1

A couple arrive at a Portuguese hotel and check in. Listen to the ⊙ 27 dialogue and see if you can pick out the various stages of the process.

Remember, you can go online to access all of the transcripts at www.collinslanguage.com/click.

Words and phrases 1

somos		we are
reservamos um quarto		we have reserved a room
senhor(a)		Mr(s)
um quarto	individual	a single room
	duplo	a double room
	com cama de casal	with a double bed
	com duas camas	with two beds (i.e. a twin room)
	com casa de banho	with an en-suite bathroom
	com duche	with a shower

noite	night
passaporte *m*	passport
cartão *m* de crédito	credit card
com certeza	of course (lit. with certainty)
aqui tem	Here you are.
elevador	lift
andar *m* – no quarto andar	storey/floor – on the fourth floor
é no primeiro andar	It's on the first floor.
pequeno-almoço *m*/tomar o pequeno-almoço	breakfast/to have breakfast
Vamos jantar a uma casa de fado.	We're going to have dinner in a **casa de fado**. **Fado** is a typical Portuguese, melancholic music usually played by two guitar players accompanying one singer.
Deseja mais alguma coisa?	Would you like anything else?

 ## Unlocking the language 1

Aqui tem.	'Here you are.' This is the response to **Dê-me ...?** in the dialogue.
Onde é ...? É ...	'Where is ...?' 'It's (located) ...' When dealing with something's location or position, remember that Portuguese uses the verb **ser** to convey the 'is' or 'it is' part of the sentence.
É à esquerda/ à direita.	'It's on the left/the right.'
sempre em frente	It's useful at this point to know how to say 'straight ahead', too
Dê-me o/a ...?	'Will you give me ...?'/'May I have ...?' This is an example of where Portuguese speakers are very direct; this is perfectly polite, unlike in English where directness can sometimes seem rude.
para dez noites	When you're booking something **for** a period of time, remember to use **para** (+ duas horas, três dias, sete noites, etc.)

Numbers 13–29

In Unit 1, we looked at numerals from 1 to 12. Here's the next batch, from 13 to 29.

13 treze
14 catorze

15 quinze

Notice the structure of the next few: e.g. 16 is composed of 'ten and six'.

16 dezasseis
17 dezassete
18 dezoito

19 dezanove
20 vinte

From 21 to 29, you'll see a structure of 'twenty and one', 'twenty and two', and so on.

21 vinte e um
22 vinte e dois
23 vinte e três
24 vinte e quatro
25 vinte e cinco

26 vinte e seis
27 vinte e sete
28 vinte e oito
29 vinte e nove

Numbers 30–99

Now let's look at higher numbers from 30 to 99. Note that in this group, the number will always be composed of three words unless it's a multiple of ten, such as 30, 40 and so on. The format is the multiple of ten + **e** ('and') + the corresponding single digit.

30 trinta
31 trinta e um
32 trinta e dois
40 quarenta
46 quarenta e seis
50 cinquenta

60 sessenta
70 setenta
80 oitenta
90 noventa
99 noventa e nove

Be careful with the similarity between 60 and 70.

Listen again to the dialogue on track 27 and check your under-standing by answering these questions: 27

1. How many nights will they be staying? ....

2. What is the room number? ....

3. What time is breakfast? ....

4. What time is dinner? ....

Find expressions in the dialogue to convey the following: 27

1. We have a room booked.

2. for ten nights

3. your passport and your credit card

4. on the first floor

5. Dinner is at seven o'clock in the evening.

6. Is there anything else you need?

7. See you later.

Pronunciation Tip

Portuguese pronunciation includes a lot of nasal sounds, which may seem unusual at first but some practice will get you there:

casa de banho, senhor

The Portuguese **nh** is pronounced rather like the 'ni' in the English 'onion' but it sounds a bit more guttural. We'll do some more practice of this sound later.

A vowel is always pronounced nasally whenever it precedes 'm'or 'n' or has a tilde (~) over it:

não, estão, são   like 'ow' in English 'owl'

com   like the 'on' in English 'wrong'

um   (oong)

sim   like the 'ng' in 'English'

tem   like the 'an' in English 'ancient'

Now, using the language you've learned think about arriving at a hotel, but this time with slightly different requirements. How would you say the following? Check your answers by listening to the audio track.

⊙ 28

1. A single room with a shower.
2. A double room with an en-suite bathroom.
3. A twin room.
4. A room with a double bed.
5. A room for fourteen nights.

· ·

Listen to the guest and make sure you have understood her requirements:

⊙ 29

1. What sort of room is mentioned? ....
2. How many nights will she be staying? ....
3. What bathroom facility is specified? ....

· ·

Match the questions on the left with the answers on the right:

Dê-me o seu passaporte, por favor?	É às oito.
Onde é o elevador?	Não, obrigado.
A que horas é o pequeno-almoço?	Fica aqui à esquerda.
Deseja mais alguma coisa?	Com certeza, aqui tem.

 ## Listen up 2

Later the same day, Claire asks the earlier receptionist's male colleague to recommend a good *casa de fado*. Listen to the dialogue.

⊙ 30

Words and phrases 2

pergunta	question
hoje	today
jantamos	we have dinner
centro *m* da cidade	city centre
recomendo	I recommend
comida *f*	food
ambiente	atmosphere
É a cinco minutos a pé.	It's five minutes on foot.
ao fundo de	at the end of
Fecha muito tarde.	It closes very late.

Unlocking the language 2

Como está?	This is a really handy little question, which can be used to enquire about someone's health, how things are going or how they are getting on with a specific task or activity. The English 'how's it going?' is possibly the broadest equivalent.
Onde são ...?/ Onde ficam ...?	Where are ...? Adding an 'm' to **fica** changes the meaning from 'it is' to the plural 'they are'. We can now contrast **Onde fica a estação?** (Where is the station?) with **Onde ficam as casas de fado?** (Where are the fado restaurants?).
a cinco metros/ a dez minutos	To say how far away something is (either in distance or in time) we need to use the little word **a** – it equates to the notion of 'away' in English: **Fica a dez kilómetros./ Daqui a dez minutos.** = It's ten kilometres./Ten minutes from here.
A que horas é? É às oito.	When you're asking what time something is or happens, remember to begin the question with **a** ('at').
Fica/É longe/perto.	'It's far away/close by.'
Não se preocupe.	'Don't worry.' This is quite a complex structure in Portuguese, but we can just learn it here as a one-off.

Can you say the following numbers in Portuguese?

1. 32
2. 44
3. 59
4. 60
5. 67
6. 76
7. 81
8. 93

. . . .

Can you say the following in Portuguese? Check your answers by listening to the audio track. ⊙ 31

1. Is it far?
2. It's ten minutes away on foot.
3. The food is very good.

. . . .

Make sure you've understood what is being said in these short dialogues. Listen out in particular for the following information: ⊙ 32

1. Where is the hotel, and how many minutes does it take to get there?
2. Is the lift on the left or the right, and how many metres away?

. . . .

Looking at the map above, complete the directions given below:

- Por favor, onde é a casa de fado?

- A casa de fado .... no
  .... da ....
  principal, à ....

. . . .

The following dialogue has one mistake in each line. Use the language you've learned above to work out what's wrong:

Tourist	Boa tarde. Onde é o casa de fado?
Receptionist	A casa de fado é no rua Augusta.

Tourist	Muita obrigado. É longe?
Receptionist	Não, está no fim da rua, à esquerda.
Tourist	Muito boa. Até logo.
Receptionist	A deus.

Let's recap

Study the following short dialogues based around what time events begin. They're just there for you to read, recognise and use for practice.

1. A que horas **é** o jantar?
   É às nove.
2. A que horas **jantamos**?
   Jantamos às oito.
3. A que horas **fecham** as casas de fado?
   Fecham à meia-noite.

Useful Tips

- notice that the verb in the question is reused in the answer!
- Remember the usage of **a** in the question and of **à** (singular)/**às** (plural) in the answer.

....

Choose the correct option to complete each sentence:

1. Bom dia. Reservámos um ....
   a. cama   b. hotel   c. quarto   d. pequeno-almoço
2. O restaurante é .... direita
   a. o   b. as   c. os   d. à
3. A que horas é o jantar? É às ....
   a. oito   b. um   c. meio-dia   d. tarde
4. Onde .... o hotel?
   a. é   b. são   c. está   d. és

Os petiscos
Out for some petiscos

We'll be looking at the popular Portuguese pastime of going out for **petiscos** as well as learning how to order drinks in a bar.

Traveller's tip

One of the greatest pleasures during your time in Portugal will be relaxing over a few leisurely petiscos in a **tasca**, taking your time to sample as wide a range as possible.

A **petisco** is a small portion of food to go with your glass of beer or wine, served at a small charge.

You can enjoy petiscos as appetisers in a restaurant or even choose from a menu in a typical Portuguese tasca, which is usually a simple bar where good food is served at low prices. Tascas are very popular with people of all ages and social backgrounds because the Portuguese like to enjoy their traditional food, wine and beer without having to spend a fortune. There are even whole guides on nothing but tascas!

You can ask for something as simple as a small tray of **tremoços** (lupin seeds) or **amendoins** (peanuts), through to **croquetes** (croquettes), **pastéis de bacalhau** (cod fish cakes) or **rissois** (rissoles)

(deep fried savoury pastries usually filled with meat or seafood), to **camarões fritos** (fried shrimps) or any number of tasty prepared snails, dog whelks, **caranguejos** (crabs), **mexilhões** (mussels), **salada de polvo** (octopus salad) or generally fish-based or meat-based titbits. Many come with a portion of bread or toast.

If you'd like more of your favourite petisco, you can order it as **um prato** (on a medium-sized plate) or for a smaller or a larger portion, as **um pires** (on a saucer) or **uma travessa** (on a tray).

We'll be learning and using several useful new verbs in this unit. These are vital for ordering petiscos and drinks.

O que tem para petiscar ...?	What petiscos do you have ...?
Este petisco tem ...?	Does this petisco contain ...?
Pode-me servir ...?	Can I have ...?

Listen up 1

A couple are in a tasca, wondering what petiscos to order. Their waiter tells them more about the dishes on the menu. Listen to the conversation, but beware: this section may get your mouth watering!

⊙ 33

Words and phrases 1

O que vão desejar?	What would you like?
Tem um menu de petiscos?	Do you have a titbits/snacks menu?
petisco *m*	titbit, snack
vejamos	let's see
O que será isto?	What is this?
É um ...	The thing is ...
Tem fiambre?	Does it contain ham? Two alternative ways of finding out what is in your food are: **Este petisco leva...?/De que e feito este petisco?** (lit. Does this snack contain...?/What is this snack made of?)
salada *f* de polvo *m*	octopus salad
Eu sou vegetariano/a.. *m/f*	I'm a vegetarian.
Não como carne.	I don't eat meat.
peixe	fish
há	There is/There are... Unlike other verbs, **há** remains the same whether the noun is singular or plural.

marisco *m*	shellfish
ou	or
pastéis *m pl* de bacalhau *m*	cod fish cakes
batata *f*	potato
salsa *f*	parsley
queria...	I would like
salada *f* de ovas *f pl*	roe salad
agora mesmo	right now (coming right up)
Pode-me trazer?	(lit: Bring me ...?/Can you bring me ...?)
um prato *m*	portion size (lit. a plate)
queijo *m*	Cheese. A popular Portuguese cheese is **Queijo Alentejano**, a mature cheese often made from goat or sheep's milk.
diferentes queijos *m pl*	different cheeses
um pouco de pão *m*	a bit of bread
E para beber?	(What can I get you) to drink?
Traga-me ...?	Can I have ...?
copo *m* de vinho *m* tinto	glass of red wine. **Copo** is used for a 'glass' of wine/spirits. **Tinto** is the word used for 'red' in this context. You can also order **vinho branco** (white), **vinho verde** (green).
da casa	house (wine, etc.)
Vou fazer o pedido, aguarde por favor.	I'll bring it out to you in just a moment. (lit. I'm going to bring the order, wait please.)
empregado *m*/empregada *f*	bartender or waiter/waitress
camarão *m*	shrimp
rissol *m*	Rissole (deep-fried savoury pastries usually filled with meat or seafood). The plural of rissole is **rissóis**.
este *m*/esta *f*	this (one)
estes *m pl*/estas *f pl*	these (ones)
cerveja *f*	beer
Sentem-se, vou trazer a comida.	Sit down. I'll bring it right over.

Unlocking the language 1

Tem ...?	Have you got ...? **Tem** is from the verb **ter** ('to have'). We also see **tem** used to refer to a petisco ('Does it have/contain ...?') and the plural **têm** ('They have/contain ...').
Traga-me ...?	(lit. Bring me ...?) This kind of direct question might sound a bit impolite for an English native speaker but is perfectly normal and adequate for a Portuguese.
Pode-me trazer ...?	However, if you feel more comfortable with it you can always add **pode-me** and ask **Pode-me trazer?** (lit. Can you me bring ...?).

Your turn 1

Match the photos with the petiscos:

1. copo de vinho tinto

2. salada de polvo

3. pão

a.   b.   c.

· ·

Find expressions in the dialogue to convey the following: 🔘 33

1. Have you got a petiscos menu?
2. Here you are.
3. I'm vegetarian (female).
4. It contains parsley and cod.
5. Can I have two shrimp rissoles?
6. Something to drink?
7. Can I have a small glass of beer, please?

Pronunciation Tip

petisco/petiscos

As we saw earlier, in Portuguese the 's' is pronounced 'sh' whenever it precedes a consonant (e.g. **petisco, estudante**) or at the end of a word.

Try to practise **petisco**: *pe-TISH* (like the 'ish' in English) *-koo*.

The plural would be: *pe-TISH-koosh* (**petiscos**).

Now, using the language you've learned above, think about 34
ordering some different petiscos and drinks. How would you say
the following? Begin each order with *Pode-me trazer ...?* Check your
answers by listening to the audio track.

1. three cod fish cakes
2. two shrimp rissoles
3. bread
4. two beers
5. a glass of white wine

....

Listen to the food and drink orders, and make sure you have 35
understood them:

1. First customer – how many pastries of each flavour are ordered? ....
   ....

2. Second customer – what does the customer order a bit of? ....

3. Third customer – is it two beers and a glass of white wine, or something different?
   ....

....

Match the expressions on the left with their translations on the right:

1. Isto tem carne?   with a bit of bread
2. com um pouco de pão   three beers
3. Pode-me trazer um pires de caracóis?   Have these got meat in them?
4. três cervejas   Can I have a saucer of snails?

 Listen up 2

In the next bar, it's time to order 36
some drinks. You'll hear an order
for both hot and cold drinks, as well
as some nibbles.

O que desejam tomar, senhores/as?	What are you having?
descafeinado *m*	decaffeinated coffee
com leite *m*	with milk. The main coffee orders in Portugal are **uma bica** (like an espresso), **um garoto** (as above, but with a small amount of milk) and **um galão** (served in a latte cup, with hot milk)
algo para petiscar	'something to pick at' – The Portuguese will often **petiscar** at appetisers before moving on to a proper meal in a restaurant. Or they will go to a **tasca** (a place where only petiscos and drinks are served) only to **petiscar**.
tenho	I have (this is another part of **ter** – to have)
azeitonas *f pl*	olives
caracóis *m pl*	snails
búzios *m pl*	dog whelks

Unlocking the language 2

tomar	This is a very useful verb, meaning 'to take', in the sense of 'consume'. You can use it to mean either 'eat' or 'drink'.
Tem alguma coisa para petiscar?	Do you have something to nibble on? The word **para** features a lot when a waiter is asking you what you want: you might hear **Para beber?** (What do you want to drink?), **Para petiscar?** (Do you want some nibbles?) or **Para comer?** (Do you want to sit down to lunch?)
Não posso comer...	You've already seen **Não como...** which means 'I don't eat...' but **Não posso comer...** is slightly different, meaning, 'I *can't* eat...' Make a note of the difference between the two and look out for further examples of these as you continue through the course.
Um pires de...	A saucer of... When you're ordering petiscos there are three sizes you can choose from. **Um pires** is the smallest portion size, **um prato** will give you a medium-sized plate and if you're still hungry you can order **uma travessa**, a tray!

Find the petiscos and drinks hidden in these anagrams:

1. isóarcac ....
2. ecrajev ....
3. sirsóis ....
4. stisépa ....
5. stisépa ....
6. oijqeu ....
7. soav ....
8. facé ....

....

Can you say the following in Portuguese? Check your answers by listening to the audio track. ⊙ 37

1. Have you got anything to nibble?
2. Can I have a portion of olives, please?

....

Make sure you've understood what is being said in these short dialogues. Focus on the following: ⊙ 38

1. What hot drinks are ordered in the first exchange? ....
2. In the second exchange, is the order for white wine and olives or red wine and snails? ....

....

Fill in the gaps in this conversation between a barman and a female customer. We've given you some first letters:

Empregado	O que d.................... tomar, senhora?
Cliente	Uma salada de polvo, por favor.
Empregado	Deseja mais alguma c.....................?
Cliente	Sim, traga-me também um pires de búzios.
Empregado	E p.................... b.....................?
Cliente	Uma cerveja.

Have a look back at the dialogue, and see if you can identify the following petiscos from their photos:

1. ....
2. ....
3. ....

a.

b.

c.

Let's recap

Remember that the main points in this unit have been:

1. asking if someone has something – **Tem um menu/uma ementa?**
2. asking if a petisco contains something – **Tem carne?**
3. ordering food and drinks – **Pode-me trazer uma cerveja?/E um pouco de pão?**

Now see how good your memory is. Can you give the Portuguese names for these petiscos and drinks?

1.

....

2.

....

3.

....

4.

....

5.

6.

....

Choose the correct option to complete each sentence:

1. Boa tarde. Pode-me trazer uma .... de polvo.

   a. restaurante   b. pires   c. salada   d. pão

2. O rissol não .... carne.

   a. és   b. têm   c. está   d. tem

3. .... vegetariano.

   a. sou   b. estou   c. tenho   d. tem

4. Pode-me trazer um café ...., por favor?

   a. cerveja   b. leite   c. com leite   d. croquete

No restaurante
In the restaurant

We'll be focusing on the restaurant experience in Portugal, looking at the language you'll need to order what you want, as well as highlighting some of the regional delicacies you might fancy trying.

Traveller's tip

Sitting down to a meal in Portugal – whether in a top-class restaurant or a humble set-menu bar – is not an experience to be rushed. A meal can last one or two hours in a restaurant, because Portuguese people like having long conversations while enjoying splendid food and wine.

It's interesting to note that dinner is eaten far later than you may be used to: it can start as late as 9pm or even 11pm and go on until after midnight!

Many visitors' first taste of Portuguese food is the legendary **prato do dia**, a daily menu offering three multi-choice courses, including certain drinks, for around 10–12€.

Higher up the market, restaurants such as Sinal Vermelho or Toma lá dá cá – both in Lisbon, in the famous Bairro Alto – have been making waves internationally for the excellence and originality of their cuisine.

If you fancy a more traditional and very typical Portuguese environment, try one of the **casas de fado** where you can enjoy traditional dishes and live fado music.

Each region of Portugal is fiercely and justifiably proud of its local dishes. In the south, grilled fish, fish soup and **Cataplanas,** a stew of fish and seafood, are typical, while the west coast specialises in **Caldeiradas de Peixe**, a different kind of fish stew, and various rice dishes. The northern regions of Portugal are famous for their meat, while in the centre of the country you can enjoy excellent **Cozido à Portuguesa**, a meat stew, or **Carne de Porco à Alentejana** and other meat dishes.

With Portugal's international reputation for wine production, you can be assured of a fine selection of robust reds, chilled whites, fruity rosés, sparkling wines or champagnes and the well-known **Vinho do Porto**, port wine, all affordably priced wherever you're visiting. **Bom apetite!** Enjoy your meal!

In this unit we'll be sitting down to a three-course lunch and using several useful new structures along the way. We'll learn more about the conventions of ordering food.

O que é ...?	What is ...?
Tem/Têm?	There is, there are/Is there? Are there?
Gostaria ...	I want ...

 Listen up 1

A couple go into a restaurant for a set-menu lunch. Listen to the conversation they have with the waiter, which takes you through the different stages of ordering a meal.

◉ 39

Words and phrases 1

É para comer?	Would you like to sit down to lunch? (lit: is it to eat?)
mesa *f*	table
por aqui	this way
como entrada	for starters
mexilhões	mussels
sopa *f*	soup

caldo *m* verde	a traditional Portuguese soup, made from green (**verde**) cabbage and potato
típica	typical
couve *f*	cabbage
quero	I want
E para a si?	And for you?
para mim, um/uma/uns/umas ...	for me, a/some
como prato principal	for the main course
lombo *m* (de porco *m*)	loin (of pork)
grelhado	grilled
batatas *f pl* fritas	French fries
Arroz *m* de Marisco *m*	shellfish rice
costas	back
E para o/a senhor/a?	For you?
bacalhau *m*	(dried) cod. You will have heard **Bacalhau à Gomes Sá** mentioned in the dialogue. This a popular Portuguese speciality, made from cod, potato and onion.
feito no forno	baked (lit. done in the oven)
garrafa *f*	bottle
água *f* sem gás *m*	still water (lit: water without gas). Sparkling water is **água com gás** (with gas).

🔓 Unlocking the language 1

Há .../Há ...?	'There is ...'/'There are ...'. Notice that this one little word serves as both a singular and a plural, as well as the question forms 'Is there ...?' and 'Are there ...?'
quero	The verb **querer** means, among other things, 'to want' – here we have **quero**, 'I want'. Don't worry about sounding too direct in saying that you 'want' something in Portuguese.
Traga-me ...	Very similar to **Dê-me ...**, this is from the verb **trazer** ('to bring') and asks the bartender to 'bring' the food or drink to the table.

Find expressions in Listen up 1 to convey the following: ◉ 39

1. Have you got a table for two? ....

2. for starters ....

3. for the main course ....

4. What is *caldo verde*? ....

5. I want the mussels. ....

6. Something to drink? ....

7. two glasses of red wine ....

Pronunciation Tip

**para, querer, prato, branco
arroz, garrafa**

The Portuguese **r** generally needs a lot of work to be
mastered. It's often said that Scots have an advantage
here, as their trilled 'rrrr' is what is required when you
want to pronounce **r**. However, the double **rr** is
pronounced like a guttural 'he' of English 'help'. Practise
rolling your **r** with as many vibrations as you can manage,
then try pairs or words with **r** and **rr**: e.g. **para** ('for', which
we've met), **caro** (which means 'expensive') and **carro**
(which means 'car'). The greatest challenge is words like
correr ('to run') and **torradeira** ('toaster') which have
one of each! For extra practice, you could try this tongue-
twister: **O rato roeu a rica roupa do rei de Roma**.
(Lit: 'The mouse gnawed the swanky clothes of the
Roman king.')

· ·

Now, using the language you've learned above, think about
ordering a range of different starters, main courses and drinks.
How would you say the following? Begin each order with *Para
mim, um ...* Check your answers by listening to the audio track.

1. shellfish rice

2. grilled loin of pork

3. traditional Portuguese soup

4. a Portuguese speciality made with cod

5. a glass of port

Listen to the customers, and make sure you have understood what 41
the orders are. Is each order true or false?

1. The order is for mussels and shellfish rice. ....

2. The order is green soup and grilled loin of pork. ....

3. The order is for one beer and a bottle of sparkling water. ....

....

Match the expressions on the left with their 'continuations' on the right:

1. Como entrada há/temos ...   água sem gás

2. Para beber quero uma ...   para quatro?

3. Depois quero um ...   salada de polvo

4. Tem uma mesa ...   arroz de marisco

The couple have finished their main courses. Their waiter asks them what they'd like next. You'll hear that the conversation covers both desserts and coffees, as well as paying at the end of their meal.

⊙ 42

Words and phrases 2

Está tudo bem?/Como está?	General use is 'How's it going?'/ 'How are things?' Here the meaning is 'How was it (the meal)?'
tudo	everything
Desejam ...?	Do you (plural) want ...? (Lit: Do you desire ...?) An alternative to this is **Querem** ...? (Lit. Do you (plural) want...?)
sobremesa *f*	dessert
gelado *m*	ice cream
bolo de bolacha	A Portuguese biscuit-cake. It's not dissimilar to the Italian dessert, tiramisu.
arroz doce	Portuguese rice pudding
pudim flan *m*	this is actually a crème caramel
Vão desejar café?	Do you (plural) want coffee?
leite creme *m*	a dessert very similar to crème brûlée
de baunilha *f*	vanilla-flavoured
de morango *m*	strawberry-flavoured. Another popular flavour you may have recognised in the dialogue is **de chocolate**, chocolate-flavoured.
Não quero nada.	I don't want anything.
Olhe, desculpe!	a polite way of attracting someone's attention. Lit. Watch, excuse me!
Traga-me a conta, por favor	Will you bring me the bill, please?

conta *f*	the bill
cêntimos	cents
Dois são de gorjeta. *f*	Two (euros) are for a tip.
Até mais ver.	See you again.
Boas férias!	Happy holidays!

🔓 Unlocking the language 2

Querem ...?	Another part of **querer** ('to want'), this asks two people politely if they want something: **Querem café?** – 'Do you want coffee?'
há/não há	Notice that the way of making a verb negative is simply to put **não** before it: **há** – 'there is'; **não há** – 'there isn't/there aren't'.
Não quero nada.	A stage on from the use of **não**, above, is to sandwich the verb between **não** and **nada**, to produce **não** quero **nada** – I don't want anything. Don't worry that it might look like an ugly double negative (I don't want nothing) – this is correct and normal in Portuguese.
Olhe, desculpe!	This is an ideal way of attracting someone's attention politely. It's actually a command form of **olhar** ('to look'), but nobody will feel ordered about if you say it to them.
Dois são de gorjeta.	'Two (euros) are for a tip.' There's no obligation to leave a tip in Portuguese bars and restaurants (people often just leave a couple of coins) but there is no harm in leaving 5–10% if you've enjoyed your meal.
A conta, por favor.	'The bill/check, please.' It's the standard – and easiest – way to ask if you can settle up, but you can also say **Traga-me a conta, por favor** (lit. Bring me the bill/check, please).

Your turn 2

Find the desserts and flavours hidden in these anagrams:

1. ogdeal ....

2. nalf ....

3. tliee mecer ....

4. ngoarmo ....

5. libunaha ....

....

Can you say the following in Portuguese? 43

1. I don't want anything, thank you. (*answer as a female*)

2. For me, an espresso.

3. Can I settle up, please?

....

Listen to these short dialogues, and identify which of the options 44
is being asked for:

1. Does the customer ask for:
   a. a coffee and a vanilla ice cream
   b. a crème brûlée and a strawberry ice cream
   c. a chocolate ice cream and some fruit

2. Does the customer ask for:
   a. two black coffees
   b. one white coffee
   c. one white coffee and a coffee with a dash of milk

....

Each line below has its words in the wrong order. Use the language you've
learned above to work out what's wrong:

1. favor conta por a?

2. tem conta a aqui

3. trinta são senhor euros

4. de dois gorjeta são

 Let's recap

Remember that the main points in this unit have been:

1. establishing what there is (on a menu) – **Há gelado de chocolate?**

2. stating preferences/orders – **Quero a caldeirada de peixe/Quero um
   pudim flan/Quero um café.**

3. looking at restaurant conventions – **uma mesa para dois; entrada/prato
   principal/sobremesa; a conta por favor?**

Now see how good your memory is. Can you give the Portuguese names for these dishes?

1. green soup
2. octopus salad
3. fish stew
4. grilled loin of pork
5. crème caramel
6. crème brûlée

a.

b.

c.

d.

e.

f.

....

Choose the correct option to complete each sentence:

1. .... prato do dia há Carne de Porco à Alentejana ou Arroz de Marisco.

   a. Por   b. Para   c. A   d. Como

2. .... sobremesa?

   a. São   b. Querem   c. Está   d. A

3. .... um garoto, por favor.

   a. Sou   b. Para mim   c. São   d. Uma

4. Dois euros são de ....

   a. mesa   b. restaurante   c. ser   d. gorjeta

....

Food and drink

It's a good idea to go back through your work and make a list of all the types of food and drink, noting any points of cultural interest. Also check over the conventions for ordering, and the things that a waiter/waitress is likely to ask you – in this way you'll be prepared when you make your first trip into a Portuguese tasca or restaurant!

Revisão 1
Revision 1

About yourself

Can you remember how to build up the following information about yourself in Portuguese, using the verb ser?

- I am (*name*)
- I am (*nationality*) – remember to use the masculine or feminine ending
- I am from (+ *town or country*)
- I am (*job/occupation*) – remember not to use an equivalent of 'a' before the job

Listen up

Listen to the voicemail left by the manager of a Portuguese property company for an English-speaking client, Mr Dobson. Then answer the questions below. ⊙ 45

Listen to the passage, which is a message left by the manager of a Portuguese property company letting out a house to an English-speaking client. To be doubly sure you've understood, listen to the passage several times with pauses, and try write down everything the man says. From your notes, answer the following questions:

1. What is the caller's full name? ....
2. Which company does he represent? ....
3. On what street is the house located, and at what number? ....
4. Who has the key – what is her full name? ....
5. What is her nationality and what language is she said to speak? ....

....

Speak out

You might like to think about where you are going for your holidays. How would you say the following in Portuguese? ⊙ 46

1. Are you going to Faro?
3. Are you going to Portugal?
2. Yes, I'm going to Faro.
4. No, I'm not going to Portugal.

Or maybe you're going somewhere this afternoon (the museum, the station, class, etc.)? How would you say the following in Portuguese?

5. Are you going to the hotel?   **6.** No, I'm going to a restaurant.

Where is ...?

Think about places and items in your life, and where they're located. Perhaps your local bar is at the end of the street on the left, or the railway station is 'near here'. In all these cases of 'location', you'll be using the verb **ser** or **ficar**. Practise asking 'Where is...?' and replying 'It's...' using **é/fica**.

Read the following short text describing a city centre, then answer the questions that follow:

A rua principal fica no centro da cidade. Tem muitas tascas e muitas lojas. Na rua há quatro restaurantes: dois italianos e dois indianos. A minha tasca preferida é a Tasca do Rossio. É no fim da rua, à esquerda. Tem petiscos muito bons.

1. Where is the main street? ....

2. How many restaurants are there, and what sort of food do they serve? ....
....

3. Where is Tasca do Rossio located? ....

4. What compliment is paid at the end? ....

At what time?

Look again at the structure for saying at what time things happen. Now try to remember how you would write the following sentences in Portuguese:

1. At what time does the train from Lisbon arrive?

2. It arrives at three o'clock.

3. At what time does the bus to Santarém leave?

4. It leaves at half past ten.

Numbers

Revise the numbers from 0 to 99 carefully. Try to spot and memorise the patterns in clusters (e.g. the teens, twenties) and the rhythm beyond 31.   ⊙ 4 7

Now try to say out loud the following numbers in Portuguese:

16   20   27   30   31   56   67   78   80   94

Falar com as pessoas
Talking to people

7

We'll go deeper into some of the structures we've already covered, to allow you to engage more fully in conversations with people you meet. We'll also learn how to speak to people in a friendlier way.

Traveller's tip

One of the trickiest barriers to overcome when you're learning Portuguese and using it to talk to people is the range of different ways of saying 'you'.

In standard modern English, there is just one form: whether you're talking to one person or ten, to a prime minister or a child, the word is simply 'you'.

In Portuguese it's different. So far in this course, we've used what is known as the formal or polite form, generally used when you don't know someone very well and you want to be respectful. This has been characterised by the word **você** (polite 'you') and a particular verb form to go with it.

In this unit we'll turn our attention to the informal, 'friendly' form, used with someone your age or younger, with whom you feel comfortable and whom you now feel you know a bit better. This is often known as the **tu** form (= informal 'you').

With practice you'll know instinctively which form to use. It's safer to start with the polite form so as not to risk offending anyone, but the Portuguese will understand that you're not being intentionally rude if you use the wrong form. They'll often put you at your ease by saying **trata-me por tu** ('speak to me informally') or **podemos tratar-nos por tu** ('we can treat each other as **tu**').

In this unit we'll be looking at formal and informal ways of addressing people. We'll also be revising some earlier structures and adapting them.

És estudante?	Are you a student?
Vais ao centro?	Are you going to the centre?
Quantos anos tens?	How old are you?

 ## Listen up 1

Tom and Linda are on the bus, and bump into a man they met the previous day. They're all on their way to do some shopping, but decide to go to a bar for a quick drink first. Listen carefully because they'll be ordering drinks and also revealing some ages! ⊙ 48

Words and phrases 1

Podemos tratar-nos por tu.	We can treat each other as **tu**.
comprar	to buy
tomar algo	to have something to drink
Pode ser	Why not? (lit. could be)
És meu convidado.	It's my treat (lit: you're invited). **Convidar** is 'to invite', and is the usual way for someone to say that they will pay for something.

olha	an informal way of attracting someone's attention (it's also a part of **olhar**- 'to see' - which we met when we learned the formal **olhe**)
É para já.	Right away.
aniversário *m*	birthday
parabéns *m pl*	congratulations
se não é indiscrição	if you don't mind my asking
Quantos anos tens?	How old are you?
Tenho vinte e três anos.	I'm 23.
Sou o velho do grupo.	I'm the old one in the group.
Não **te** preocupe**s**.	Don't worry (we saw the formal **não se preocupe** in another unit).
Brindemos! Saúde!	Cheers! (lit: let's drink to someone's health)

Unlocking the language 1

Vais ao centro?
Queres tomar algo? Como estás?

We're now starting to focus on the informal style of each verb. Generally, this is just the formal 'you' style we've learned (**tem, quer, vai**) with an **-s** added on (**tens, queres, vais**). We'll do plenty more practice, so don't worry if it's a bit confusing at first.

Dá-me três cervejas, por favor.

Here's the informal way of asking for drinks. You can now compare it with the formal **Dê-me ...**

o aniversário de Linda

There's no apostrophe in Portuguese to allow us to say something like 'Linda's birthday'. Instead, we have to say 'the birthday of Linda'.

Quantos anos tens?
Tenho vinte e três anos.

To ask and tell our age in Portuguese, we don't talk about being 23, but rather having 23 years. So we use the verb **ter** – **Quantos anos tens?** (How many years do you have?); **tenho vinte e três anos** (I have 23 years).

Find expressions in the dialogue (track 48) to convey the following: ⊙ 48

1. We can treat each other as **tu**.
2. Are you going to the centre?
3. Do you want something to drink?
4. It's my treat.
5. Congratulations!
6. Don't worry.

> **Pronunciation Tip**
>
> **hoje, hotel**
>
> Note that the letter **h** in Portuguese is used in writing but is never pronounced (it's a silent consonant). As you will hear, the words **hoje** ('today') and **hotel** are pronounced **oje** and **otel**.

· ·

Speaking informally and using dar, how would you ask for the following? ⊙ 49

Can I have ...

1. ... three beers, please?
2. ... two glasses of red wine, please?
3. ... a portion of olives, please?

· ·

Listen to the people talking and focus on the following questions: ⊙ 50

1. How old is the first speaker?
2. The second speaker says 'you are 15' – is the address formal or informal?
3. How old is the third speaker?

· ·

Formal or informal? Complete the table below, supplying the informal bits of each verb. We've given you one to start off:

Formal	Informal
Quantos anos tem?	Quantos anos tens?
Dê-me uma cerveja, por favor?	....
Quer uma dose de batatas?	....
Vai ao centro?	....
Prefere ir ao museu?	....
Está nervoso?	....

Listen up 2

Sofia chats to a foreign student in the park. **Listen out for details of their jobs and studies.**

◉ 51

Words and phrases 2

Desculpa	Excuse me – informal command from **desculpar** (to excuse). You've already seen the formal form **desculpe** used in Unit 3.
perdido/a *m/f*	lost
Não és de cá, pois não?	You're not from here, are you?
és	you are (from **ser**)
canadiano/a *m/f*	Canadian
estar de férias *f pl*	To be on holiday. To go on holiday is **ir de férias.**
estudo	I study (from **estudar**)
escola *f* de línguas *f pl*	language school
falas	you speak (from **falar**)
praticar	to practise
és minha convidada	it's my treat (lit. you're my guest)
Então	then

guia	person working as. This is the feminine form of **És meu convidado** that you saw in Words and Phrases 1. A guide (**guia** can work for both a man and a woman)
emprego/trabalho *m*	job/work
trabalhar	to work
pouco tempo *m* livre	very little free time
prefiro	I prefer
pedir	to order (drinks/food)/to ask (for)
alguma coisa	something
sumo *m* de laranja *f*	orange juice (lit: juice of orange)

🔒 Unlocking the language 2

estás perdido?
estou bem
estás de férias?

Have a look at the various usages of **estou** and **estás**. Remember that while **ser** is used for personal issues like our name, nationality and job, **estar** is used to describe the location of something, to describe how you're feeling – a temporary state or condition (excited, tired, bored, etc.)

és estudante
Não és de cá, pois não?
sou canadiano
sou professora e guia

Now look at the usages of **ser**, and make sure you understand why **estar** is not used.

és

This is the informal 'you' form of **ser**. Let's summarise this verb a bit:
sou – I am
és – you are (informal)
é – you are (polite)

gosto de trabalhar

The **gosto de** structure works not only with things (**gosto de futebol/de arte**) but also with activities expressed as verbs: **gosto de trabalhar** (I like working – lit: I like to work).

Que interessante!

This phrase actually means, 'How interesting!'. This construction is often used to remark on something. You can create your own phrases like this using other adjectives, for example: **Que bom!** or **Que bonito!**

Here are some anagrams of some informal Portuguese verbs (ending in -s), for you to unravel:

1. sfaal ....
2. somat ....
3. resque ....
4. nset ....
5. isav ....
6. sé ....

Can you say the following in Portuguese? Check your answers by listening to the audio track.   ⊙ 52

1. Are you on holiday? (*informal*)
2. I'm on holiday.
3. I'm fine.
4. Don't worry. (*informal*)

Listen to the four descriptions (A, B, C and D) and match what is said in each case with the corresponding photo: ⊙ 53

1.

....

2.

....

3.

4.

....

....

Below are some formal (polite) questions. Use the language you've learned in this unit to change each verb to the informal style:

1. Quer tomar um café?
2. Tem muito tempo livre?
3. Prefere ir a um museu ou a um restaurante?
4. Vai ao centro da cidade?

Let's recap

In this unit we've looked at the difference between polite and informal ways of addressing people. We've also studied the way to ask and state how old someone is. Here are some model sentences to help you remember:

(Você) É canadiano? (*polite*)

És canadiano? (*informal*)

(Você) Quer ir a um jogo de futebol? (*polite*)

Queres ir a um jogo de futebol? (*informal*)

(Você) Quantos anos tem? (*polite*)

Quantos anos tens? (*informal*)

Tenho trinta e quatro anos. ('I' – *first person singular*)

Now see how good your memory is for numbers. Each of the numbers below is misspelt. Try to spot the error then practise saying the corrected version.

1. 33   trinta e tres
2. 44   quaranta e quatro
3. 55   quinquenta e cinco
4. 66   sesenta e seis

....

Choose the correct option to complete each sentence:

1. Tu .... nervoso.
   a. és   b. é   c. está   d. estás
2. Tu .... 23 anos.
   a. és   b. tens   c. é   d. tem
3. Tu .... ir ao museu.
   a. tem   b. tens   c. quer   d. queres
4. Tu .... que ir ao museu.
   a. tem   b. tens   c. quer   d. queres

Ir às compras
Out shopping

We'll cover the language you'll need when you go out shopping, and take a look at what sorts of shops you can expect to find.

Traveller's tip

At some point in your trip to Portugal, you're bound to fancy a saunter around the shops to see what's on offer and perhaps pick up a bargain.

The textile industry is one of the most important in the field of Portuguese exports. The first thing you'll notice in Portuguese cities is the quantity of shopping centres (each is called a **centro comercial**) in which large chains and designer shops are present. In Lisboa you can find Europe's largest, **O Colombo**.

If you head downtown, you will also find the more traditional, family-run shops and small businesses. If you're looking for a bargain, try a **feira** ('textile market') which usually takes place every week or every month on a specific date.

There are also a variety of other markets such as **feiras de artesanato** (craft markets), which take place regularly, and **feiras de antiguidades** (antique markets) in Algés and Oeiras (Lisbon) at weekends. Two other markets - the Feira da Ladra (thieves' market) with a wide range of second-hand items, taking place on Tuesdays and Saturdays, and the Feira do Relógio, on Sundays - are comparable on a smaller scale to those in Portobello Road and Camden Town in London. These markets usually end during the afternoon, at around 3 or 4pm.

Store opening hours are generally quite long, with most stores staying open until 7pm, or even till 10pm or midnight in shopping centres. Be aware that most smaller shops close for lunch, usually between about 1.30pm and 2.30pm.

Whether you're a shopaholic or a retail novice, a dip into the sights, noise and smells of Portuguese shopping is always a colourful experience.

In this unit we'll be revising some of the structures we met in earlier units, and will look carefully at the language you'll need to browse and make purchases.

Tem ...?   Have you got ...?
Quero/prefiro   I want/I prefer
More numbers

 Listen up 1

Stephanie is looking to buy a shirt for herself. Listen to the dialogues to see how she gets on. Try to pick out the price of the item she buys.

⊙ 54

' ' Words and phrases 1

O que procura?	What are you looking for? **procurar** is 'to look for' – you don't need an extra word for 'for'.
Procuro	I'm looking for...
blusa *f* / camisa *f* / casaco *m*	blouse/shirt/jacket
branco/branca *m/f*	white
(de) algodão *m*	(made of) cotton
tamanho *m*	size (of shirt, etc.)
médio	medium
Posso prová-la?	Can I try it on?
claro que sim	of course
Como lhe fica?	How does it look?/How is it (on you)?
Fica um pouco pequena/apertada.	It's a bit small/tight.

Não vou levar/Vou deixá-la.	I'll leave it.
só um momento	just a moment
É um pouco cara.	It's a bit expensive.
outro/outra *m/f*	other/another. You don't need an additional word for 'an' – '(an)other' is included in **outro** and **outra**.
bonito/bonita *m/f*	pretty
Eu vou levá-la/Vou comprá-la.	I'll take it/buy it.
Passe pela caixa, para pagar, por favor.	Come to the till (lit: to pay), please.

🔓 Unlocking the language 1

Posso prová-la?
Vou levá-la.

The various structures with the words **-la** and **-lo** are quite complex, so it's best here just to study the two usages and learn the expressions as they appear. Just remember, use **-la** when you are refering to something in the feminine (**a** blusa » levá-**la**), use **-lo** for the masculine (**o casaco** » levá-**lo**).

Adjectives

You'll notice that in **Words and phrases**, above, we've given you **branco** and **branca** for 'white'. Which one you use depends again on whether the item being described is masculine or feminine. **Blusa** is feminine, so we say **uma blusa branca**. A white sweater (masculine) would be **um pulôver branco**. You'll get used to it with practice.

this (one)

There's also a masculine/feminine thing going on here. 'This shirt' (feminine) is **esta blusa**, but 'this pullover' (masculine) would be **este pulôver**. If you don't want to repeat the word **blusa** and prefer to say 'this one', you can use **esta**. You can find this last variant five lines from the end of the dialogue.

O que...?/Que...?

'What ...?' You may have noticed that in certain cases you hear **O que...?** at the beginning of a 'what' question and in other cases you hear **Que...?** Don't worry too much about the rules for now – you'll be understood whichever you choose to use.

Find expressions in the dialogue to convey the following: ◎ 54

1. What are you looking for?
2. Here's one.
3. Can I try it on?
4. I'll leave it, thanks.
5. Is it cotton?
6. I'll take it.

Pronunciation Tip

O que procura?, O que quer?

As is the case in standard English, the **q** in Portuguese always comes in the combination **qu**. However, it's mostly pronounced not as the English 'queen' or 'quick', but rather like the 'k' in 'Ken'. Try pronouncing the question **O que quer?**

It's time to revise our numbers so that we can state and understand prices. How would you say the following prices? Begin each sentence with *São* and end it with *euros*. ◎ 55

1. 19 ....
2. 24 ....
3. 35 ....
4. 47 ....
5. 58 ....

Listen to the people talking, and make sure you have understood what each person is saying. Then answer the following questions: ◎ 56

1. What problem does the first speaker have? ....
2. Does the second shopper buy the item? ....
3. What does the shop assistant ask the shopper to do in the third example?

   ....

Match the English expressions on the left with their Portuguese translations on the right:

1. I'll take it.   Que tamanho procura?
2. What size are you looking for?   É um pouco cara.
3. Can I try it on?   Vou levá-la.
4. It's a bit expensive.   Posso prová-la?

It's time for more shopping, and there are some more decisions to be made. In the first dialogue the shop assistant is using the polite form of address, while in the second dialogue, the customer and the shop assistant are comfortable using the tu **form.**

⊙ 57

Words and phrases 2

prato *m*	plate
Qual?	Which one?
prefere(s)/prefiro	you prefer/I prefer
Quer que embrulhe?	'Shall I wrap that up for you?' You may sometimes be asked **É para oferta?** (Is it a gift for someone?) so that the shop assistant can gift-wrap it beautifully for you at no extra cost.
muito gentil	(that's) very kind (of you)
sapatos *m*	shoes
Como pagas?	How are you paying?
em dinheiro	In cash. Strictly speaking, foreigners in Portugal should have their passport ready when using a credit card in a shop.
Marca o teu código secreto.	Tap in your PIN (secret number). The formal variant would be **marque o seu ...** It's also common now to hear **marque o seu** (or **marca o teu**) **pin**.
Já está.	That's it – done.
não são?	aren't they? just like we do in English with the tags 'isn't it?', 'can't she?', 'shouldn't I?', etc.
lindo/a/os/as	gorgeous

Prefiro/preferes

We've got used to seeing pairs of verb forms, where the one ending in **-o** means 'I do' and the other one means 'you do': e.g. **quero** (I want) and **queres** (you want). Here's another pair, belonging to the verb **preferir** (to prefer).

Plural adjectives

You'll have noticed that we've said **estes sapatos** for 'these shoes'. Just as 'this' become 'these' in English, Portuguese has a means of denoting plurals: **este** (this) becomes **estes** (these) and the feminine **esta** (this) becomes **estas** (these). Notice also that whereas the **blusa** in the first dialogue was **bonita**, the **sapatos** here are **bonitos**. It all matches up!

Quanto são?

You are already familiar with **Quanto é?** (How much is it?) **Quanto são?** simply means How much are they? So if you are buying **um prato** you would use **Quanto é?** whereas if you were buying **dois pratos** you would say **Quanto são?**

✈ Your turn 2

Think about the use of *branco, branca, brancos, brancas* to describe things as being white. Which would be the correct form in each of the cases below?

1. um prato ....

2. uma blusa ....

3. pratos ....

4. blusas ....

· ·

Can you say the following in Portuguese? We're using the polite form. Check your answers by listening to the audio track.   ◎ 58

1. Which do you prefer?   3. in cash

2. Shall I wrap it up for you?

· ·

Make sure you've understood what is being said in these short dialogues. Look specifically for the following information: ◎ 59

1. How much is the item in the first exchange? ....

2. How will the second shopper be paying? ....

Each line below has its words in the wrong order. Use the language you've learned above to work out what's wrong:

1. seu o favor código por secreto marque ....

2. passaporte dê-me seu o ....

3. lindos estes são sapatos ....

Let's recap

Remember that the main points in this unit have been:

1. stating what you're looking for in a shop – **procuro uma blusa branca**

2. wanting and preferring – **quero esta camisa/prefiro este pulôver**

3. work on 'this/these' – **este pulôver/esta blusa/estes sapatos/estas blusas**

. . . .

Now see how good your memory is. Thinking about a shirt (uma camisa), how would you say the following?

1. I want a shirt.

2. I want a white shirt.

3. I prefer this shirt.

4. It's pretty.

. . . .

Choose the correct option to complete each sentence:

1. .... camisas são lindas.

   a. Este   b. Esta   c. Estes   d. Estas

2. Prefiro .... pratos.

   a. este   b. esta   c. estes   d. estas

3. .... pulôver é bonito.

   a. Este   b. Esta   c. Estes   d. Estas

4. Quero .... camisa.

   a. este   b. esta   c. estes   d. estas

Um pouco de cultura
A bit of culture

9

We'll take a trip to a Portuguese museum, looking at what's on offer, what you can expect to pay, and how to say what you need to say there.

Traveller's tip

Once you've had your initial burst of **petiscos** and shopping, it's time to check out the wealth of historical and contemporary cultural options on offer. Your hotel or the tourist information office will have leaflets telling you where to head for.

In fact, Portuguese cities have so much history visible in their streets and buildings that it's not always necessary to visit a museum to get your culture fix. You can plan your day to take in strolls around particular **bairros** (districts/quarters), where you can not only savour the flavour of an area, but also stop off for a **menu do dia** or a few **petiscos**.

The larger cities, especially Lisboa, Porto, Évora, Santarém, Coimbra and Guimarães, have a huge range of art galleries (**galerias**) and museums (**museus**) to cover all tastes. Look out for one of various types of city card, giving you discounted entry into certain museums. Having said that, you'll find admission prices are reasonable in Portugal, and a good number of buildings are free to enter.

As is the case with shopping, you'll find museum opening times are generous, allowing you to absorb the contents without feeling rushed. If you fancy staying on to have something to eat in the gallery's restaurant (as you can at CCB in Lisboa) – perhaps on a terrace overlooking the city – then so much the better.

In this unit we'll learn three new structures: saying that we like something, that we're going to do something, and that we want to do something.

Gosto ...	I like ...
Vou visitar ...	I'm going to visit ...
Quero ir a/ao ...	I want to go to ...

Listen up 1

A tourist is at the hotel reception desk asking for advice about a museum. We learn about the museum's location, its opening hours and admission price. See if you can pick these out as you listen.

⊙ 60

Words and phrases 1

Quero ir /Quer ir?	I want to go/Do you want to go?
museu *m*	museum
arte moderna	modern art
claro que é possível	of course it's possible
para si	for you
vou apontar	I'm going to jot down
direção *f*	directions (lit. direction)
papel *m*	(sheet of) paper. In the dialogue you will have heard **num papel, this means** on the paper.
simpático/a *m/f*	nice
lá	there/over there
Gosta ...?	Do you like ...?

Gosto (muito)	I like it (a lot)
eu também	so do I/me too
entrada *f*	admission; entry
desconto *m*	discount
abre	it opens
está aberto	it is open
desde as dez da manhã	from 8am
até às seis da tarde	until 5pm
ver	to see
muitas coisas	many things
dar uma volta	to go for a stroll
hoje	today

🔓 Unlocking the language 1

Quero ir

I want to go. Up to now, we've seen **quero** used with an item – **quero um gelado** (I want an ice cream). You can also use it with another verb to state what you want to do – **quero ir** (I want to go). You will have also heard quero ir **à** and quero ir **ao** which both mean I want to go *to*. If the noun is masculine you use ao: **quero ir ao museu** and if the noun is feminine you use **à**: **quero ir à galeria**.

Vou

Similarly, you can talk about what you're going to do by using a part of **ir** (e.g. **vou** – I'm going) + another verb, e.g. **vou tomar um café** (I'm going to have a coffee), **vou agora** (I'm going now).

Vou-lhe

If you're going to do something for someone you add **-lhe** after the verb when speaking formally: **vou-lhe apontar** (lit.: I am going for you to jot down.). If you're treating the person with **tu**, you add **-te** after the verb: **vou-te apontar**.

se for possível

If it's possible. It's best to learn this expression as a one-off. You use it when whatever is possible hasn't happened yet.

Gosta ...?
Gosto ...

Gostar is often thought of as being the verb 'to like' but it actually means 'to please', so in Portuguese, to say you like coffee, you have to turn it round and say that coffee pleases you. That explains the order of **Gosta de arte?** – Does art please you? Similarly, **Gosto de arte** suggests that art is pleasing to me (i.e. I like it). You can add **muito** for 'very much', or if you don't like (e.g. coffee), it would be **Não gosto de café**.

Find expressions in the dialogue (track 60) to convey the following: ◉ 60

1. I want to go to the museum.

2. I'm going to jot down the directions.

3. That's very kind of you.

4. Do you like modern art?

5. Yes, I like it a lot.

6. There's a discount with this card.

7. Now I'm going to go for a stroll.

Pronunciation Tip

museu, euro

Note that the letter **e** in Portuguese together with **u** – **eu** – is pronounced as one sound: mu-**SEU** (like the 'e' in English 'shed' with the 'oo' in English 'hoover').

· ·

Let's have a look at the new structures we've learned in Unlocking ◉ 61
the language above. How would you say the following? There are
some hints provided in brackets.

1. I want to go to the art gallery. (*à galeria de arte*)

2. I'm going to have a glass of wine. (*tomar um copo de vinho*)

3. I like art. (*de arte*)

· ·

Quando está aberto? Match the opening times in the left-hand column
with the corresponding figures on the right:

O CCB está aberto das oito às oito.   10.00–18.00

O Mosterio dos Jerónimos está aberto das dez às cinco.   10.00–17.30

O Museu Nacional de Arte Contemporânea está aberto das dez   8.00–20.00
às seis.

A Casa do Fado e da Guitarra Portuguesa está aberta das dez às   10.00–17.00
cinco e meia.

Mosteiro dos Jerónimos

Listen to the people talking, and make sure you have understood ⊙ 62
what they are saying. Pay particular attention to the following:

1. What does the first person like and dislike?

2. What building is the second person going to visit?

3. Where does the third person want to go?

 ## Listen up 2

During his visit to a museum, Mike buys his entry ticket, gets some ⊙ 63
assistance from a guide and later strikes up a conversation with a
female visitor. Listen to the dialogues.

Words and phrases 2

adulto *m*/adulta *f*	adult
então	so/therefore
vinte por cento	20%
contemporâneo/a	contemporary
secção *f*	section
grande	big
na ala *f* principal	in the main hall
folheto *m*	leaflet
escultura *f*	sculpture
entendido/a *m/f*	expert
exposição *f*	exhibition
comentário *m*	commentary – it can also mean simply 'comment'.
sala	room
apreciar	to appreciate/to enjoy
amável	kind
restante	rest/remainder
seguir	to follow/to continue/to carry on

Encontramo-nos	**Encontrar** the infinitive form of the verb means 'to meet/to find'. If you add **–nos** (encontramo-nos) it means 'to meet up' (lit: meet with us). So here Ana is saying 'Shall we meet at 3.00?'
Até às três.	See you at 3.00 (lit: until 3.00)

 ## Unlocking the language 2

vamos/
encontramo-nos

These are verb forms indicating that 'we' are doing the action. Let's take a moment to summarise the various 'persons' of some of the main verbs we've met:

	I	you	we
ser	sou	és	somos
estar	estou	estás	estamos
ter	tenho	tens	temos
ir	vou	vais	vamos
querer	quero	queres	queremos
preferir	prefiro	preferes	preferimos

Gostas de...

Did you recognise the informal 'you' form of **gostar** ('to like')?

 ## Your turn 2

Use the words below to fill the gaps. It's an informal dialogue:

é   *hoje*   *há*   *queres*   *encontramo-nos*   *gostas*

.... uma exposição de arte .... no museu. ....
muito interessante. .... de arte? .... ir? .... às
onze.

• •

Can you say the following in Portuguese?   ⊙ 64

1. I prefer sculpture.
2. I'm not an expert (*male*).
3. Shall we meet here at two o'clock?

Make sure you've understood what is being said in these short dialogues.

First dialogue:

1. How much is it to get in? ....

2. What discount is offered with the card? ....

Second dialogue:

3. Until what time is the building open? ....

· ·

Each line below has its words in the wrong order. Use the language you've learned above to work out what's wrong:

1. ao ir contemporânea quero de museu arte ....

2. escultura não mas sou gosto um em entendido ....

3. uma há duas às exposição ....

 Let's recap

In this unit we've looked at what we want to do, what we are going to do, and what we like. Here are some model sentences to help you remember:

(não) gosto (muito) de arte moderna

(não) quero ir ao museu

vou visitar uma galeria

· ·

Choose the correct option to complete each sentence:

1. Tem .... por cento de desconto.

   a. grande   b. dez   c. este   d. não

2. O museu não .... aberto hoje.

   a. sou   b. estou   c. é   d. está

3. Quanto .... a entrada?

   a. sou   b. euros   c. é   d. são

4. Quero .... muitas coisas.

   a. estar   b. ver   c. museu   d. ir

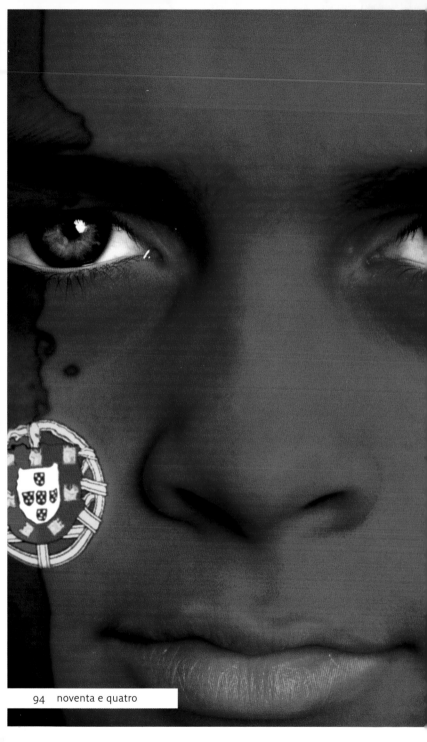

Vamos ao futebol
Off to the football

10

We'll look at the language you'll need to buy a ticket for a Portuguese football match, as well as learning something about the country's biggest sporting rivalry!

Traveller's tip

Any fixture between Benfica and Sporting is not just a football match – it's a battle between two historical rivals which is already in its centenary. Traditionally Benfica was seen as the people's team and Sporting as the aristocrats' one. Nowadays there is no real class division and the more than 200,000 members between the two clubs come from various social groups. Both teams are based in the capital, geographically practically facing each other, and the passion whipped up every time they meet is something to behold.

Equally feisty – and for similar reasons – is any game between Porto in the north and either of the big Lisboa teams. But the **o clássico** derby is still between Benfica and Sporting.

You'll struggle to get a ticket for many of the biggest encounters but, on less extreme occasions, it's relatively easy to get a ticket to see a first division match. You can check out a club's website for details of fixtures and prices, or visit the ground a day or so before the game and look for a **bilheteira** to buy your tickets.

The default kick-off time is around 7pm on a Saturday or Sunday, but TV obligations mean that there are usually a couple of games on a Saturday night (sometimes starting as late as 9.15pm) and later into Sunday evening. Check in the press or ask at the tourist information office.

Inside the ground, you'll notice that trouble is extremely rare, and that there is some chanting but far less 'singing' than you might be used to. Be prepared to join the rest of the crowd in a cry of 'gooooooloooo' when the home team scores!

In this unit we'll be revising some of the structures we've learned in earlier units, including directions, prices and times. We'll also look at a couple of twists on existing verbs, and will be learning some useful exclamations.

Como vou para o estádio de futebol?	How do I get to the football stadium?
Tem que ...	You have to ...
A que horas é o jogo?	What time is the match?
O avançado é muito bom.	The striker is very good.

Listen up 1

Tom is a real footy fan back home, so he wants to see a match during his holiday in Portugal. He asks a passer-by for directions to the football stadium. Listen out for a mode of transport and a distance in metres.
⊙ 66

Tom buys some tickets for the match at the stadium ticket office. Can you pick out the price, and the time the match kicks off?
⊙ 67

Outside the stadium, Tom asks a scarf-seller for directions. They are both young, so they speak to each other informally using **tú**.
⊙ 68

〝 Words and phrases 1

estádio *m* de futebol *m*	football stadium
tem que	you have to
apanhar	to take/catch (public transport)
depois	after
jogo *m*	game/match
bilhete *m*	ticket. You are already familiar with the word **bilhete** in the context of travel, but it can also mean entry to an event, or, as we saw in Unit 9, a museum. In this context **público** describes any ticket for non-members and **para sócios** would be for members only.

bancada *f*	seats/stands
no piso zero	on the ground floor – note, on the first or second floor would be **no piso 1 ou 2** respectively.
se tiver	if you've got (any)
são no total	in total it costs... (lit. they are in total)
cachecol *m*	scarf
do clube	club/team
dá-me	Give me – an informal command form, but it's courteous and normal, nonetheless.

Tem que apanhar ...	You have to catch ... We've seen plenty of usages of **tem**, but this is a new one. When a part of **ter** is followed immediately by **que**, the meaning shifts to obligation: not 'to have' but 'to have to (do something)'.
É às cinco.	To say that something 'is' (in the sense of 'takes place' or 'happens') at a particular time, we use the verb **ser** – hence **O jogo é às cinco**.
se tiver	If you've got (any). It's best to learn this expression as a one-off. You use it when someone might not have something.
dá-me	This is an informal command form of **dar** ('to give'). Don't worry about ordering people to do things in this way – it's completely normal in Portuguese. You can always add **por favor** if it makes you feel more comfortable.

Find expressions in the dialogues to convey the following: ◉ 66–68

1. To get to the football stadium, please? ....
2. What time is the game? ....
3. I want two tickets, please. ....
4. That's 30 euros in total. ....
5. Here on the left, 50 metres away. ....
6. Give me two. ....

Pronunciation Tip

avançado, preguiçoso, ceguinho

The Portuguese **c** is usually pronounced like the 'c' in English 'company'. However, when it is followed by an **e** or **i**, it is pronounced softly like 'c' in English 'trace'. Sometimes you find a **c** with a little mark underneath, **ç**, called a 'cedilla' (**cedilha**). This forces it to be pronounced softly, even if it is not followed by an **e** or **i** (**ça, ço, çu**). Note that in combination with **e** and **i** (**ce, ci**) it will never have a cedilla because it is pronounced softly anyway. Try to speak out loud: a-van-**ÇA**-do.

· ·

Look at the three sentences below, then find their Portuguese equivalents in the dialogue. Try to memorise the Portuguese expressions, then say them out loud: ◉ 69

1. How do I get to the football stadium? ....
2. What time is the match? ....
3. I want two tickets, please. ....

· ·

Listen to the people talking, and make sure you have understood what the people are saying: ◉ 70

1. When is the match taking place?
2. How many tickets are bought?
3. Which means of public transport is recommended to get to the stadium?

Onde fica? Look at the directions in the left-hand column and write the English versions on the right. The map below may help you.

a. Fica no fim da rua.

b. Fica à esquerda, a oitenta metros.

c. Fica perto daqui.

d. Fica aqui à direita.

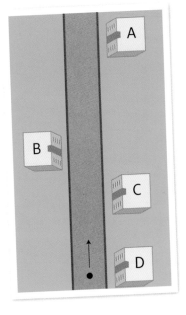

 ## Listen up 2

Inside the stadium just before the game, Tom and Rachel chat to the man in the next seat. He's a bit older than them, so they use the polite form. You'll hear some comments as they go through the game and a quick summing-up at the end.

⊙ 71

O que acha do/da ...?	What do you think of ...?
maravilhoso/a *m/f*	fantastic
vocês	you (plural of você)
equipa *f*	team
melhor	better
vamos ver	let's see
o que acontece	what happens
fora de jogo	offside
O que se passa?	What's going on?
árbitro *m*	referee
Deve ser ceguinho!	He must be blind!
nervoso/a *m/f*	nervous
golo *m*	goal
não se preocupe	don't worry
normalmente	normally
marcam	they score
Que bom!	Great!
Oxalá!	If only!
pontapé *m* de canto *m*	a corner. **É pontapé de canto** would be we've got a corner.
avançado *m*	striker
bocado	bit
preguiçoso/a *m/f*	lazy
enfim	anyway
conseguimos	we've got/we've managed to get
ponto *m*	point
Até ao próximo jogo.	See you at the next game!
Até à próxima	See you again soon!
próximo	next

O que acha do/da ...?

What do you think of ...? A great way of asking someone their opinion on what follows – in this case **do estádio** ('the stadium').

vocês

Simply the plural form of **você** – Manuel is addressing both Tom and Linda, so rather than **você é**, he says **vocês são**.

estou nervoso

Earlier in the course we learned to express 'I am' as **sou** for personal issues like our name, nationality, job and so on. But if you want to describe how you're feeling – a temporary state or condition (angry, tired, bored), you'd say **estou** – **estou nervoso**.

é preguiçoso

The striker is referred to as lazy using **é preguiçoso**, as it's deemed to be a characteristic – as opposed to the temporary state/condition we described above.

o minuto oitenta e nove

It's 'the minute 89' in football, rather than 'the 89th minute' as in English.

Oxalá!

A great little expression, which is flexible enough to mean 'if only', 'let's hope so', 'chance would be a fine thing', etc.

Here are some anagrams of Portuguese words associated with a football match, for you to unravel.

1. gojo ....
2. ebelhit ....
3. chacloce ....
4. rátibor ....
5. olog ....

Can you say the following in Portuguese? Check your answers by listening to the audio track.

 72

1. I want to see a goal.

2. offside

3. We've got a corner.

4. goal!

Make sure you've understood what is being said in the expressions 73 you'll hear:

1. Which player in the team is mentioned by his number, and what is the speaker's opinion of him?

2. Does the speaker like the stadium?

3. How many points have we won in the match?

4. What is the meaning of the fourth speaker's farewell?

∙∙

Each line below has its words in the wrong order. Use the language you've learned above to work out what's wrong:

1. do acha o estádio que? ....

2. pouco um avançado o preguiçoso é. ....

3. cachecóis favor por dois dá-me. ....

Let's recap

In this unit we've looked at what we have to do, and the difference between what we are characteristic and geographical factors (*ser*), versus temporary factors (*estar*). Here are some model sentences to help you remember:

Tenho que apanhar o metro.

Sou escocês, sou de Edimburgo, sou artista, sou alto (tall), **sou inteligente** (intelligent).

Estou nervoso, estou no estádio.

∙∙

Now see how good your memory is. Each of the sentences below has one error. Try to spot it, then practise saying the corrected version.

1. Quero ir a estádio.

2. O jogo é à cinco.

3. O avançado é muito boa.

4. Dá-me dois bilhete, por favor.

5. Gosta muito da equipa.

Choose the correct option to complete each sentence:

1. O estádio .... maravilhoso.

   a. está   b. são   c. estão   d. é

2. Hoje .... um bocado nervoso.

   a. sou   b. estou   c. somos   d. são

3. A que horas .... o jogo?

   a. está   b. onde   c. é   d. são

4. Onde .... o estádio?

   a. são   b. metro   c. ser   d. fica

A vida noturna
Nightlife

11

We'll consider some options for extending your days in Portugal into the night. Having had petiscos in Unit 5 and a meal in Unit 6, we'll now be paying a visit to a lounge bar for a nightcap and a bit of live jazz.

Traveller's tip

We've all heard stories of revellers coming back from the Algarve or Lisboa and boasting about how late they were able to stay out drinking. In fact, away from the tourist areas, the purpose of Portugal's relatively relaxed licensing laws is to allow people to unwind gently, unhurriedly, having taken in a good meal beforehand. Eating and drinking generally go hand in hand, and can make the evening far more enjoyable than just a binge.

Normal bars in cities will generally start to shut down between 11pm and 2am. After this, many Portuguese will head for what is known as **um pub** – a term borrowed from the English (though pronounced closer to 'paff') and used to denote what we might call a lounge bar. Pubs will generally close after 1am – sometimes as late as 3am or 4am – and will allow you to relax with a drink in comfortable surroundings, often listening to live

or recorded music.

Afterwards people usually go to the disco – **discoteca** is the Portuguese name, where you can stay dancing and drinking until 8am or later.

It's worth noting that Portugal's public smoking policy requires pubs and bars to declare themselves smoking or non-smoking. Some have designated areas devoted to each preference.

In this unit we'll be learning the language of making suggestions, and also looking at ways of saying what events are happening.

Vamos a um pub?	Shall we go to a lounge bar?
Porque é que não vamos tomar algo?	Why don't we have a drink?
Esta noite vai haver música ao vivo.	There's a band playing tonight.

 ## Listen up 1

Katie and Ben are with their new friend António and they're wondering what to do after dinner. See if you can pick out where they head for.

A little later on, they're lucky enough to find a bar with live music.

⊙ 74

⊙ 75

Words and phrases 1

O que queres fazer agora?	What do you want to do now?
Não sei.	I don't know.
Podemos ir tomar um copo.	We could (lit: we can) have a drink.
Conheces algum sítio?	Do you know a place?
Porque é que não vamos?	Why don't we go?
esta noite f	tonight
Entramos neste pub?	Shall we go in to this pub?
jazz m	jazz
Uau!	Great! Fantastic! Cool! (etc.)

se quiseres	Lit: If you (*informal*) want. It's best to learn this expression as a one-off. You use it to make a suggestion.
senta-te	sit down/sit yourself down
mesa *f*	table
vamos ao bar *m*	we'll go/let's go to the bar/counter
O que queres tomar?	What would you like to drink?
gin *m* com água tónica *f*/ gin-tónico *m*	gin and tonic
com muito gelo *m*	with a lot of ice
E para....?	And for...?
Podemos pedir para ele ...	We can order ... for him.
um copo de vinho do Porto	a glass of port (very famous Portuguese liqueur wine)
boa ideia	good idea

 ## Unlocking the language 1

Podemos ... Porque é que não ...?	We can/could ... Why don't we ...? These are standard ways in Portuguese of making suggestions as to what we can do. **Podemos** comes from the verb **poder** ('to be able', incorporating ideas of 'can', 'could', etc.). It's used for 'can' in terms of permission (**podemos entrar** – we're allowed to go in) and in many contexts of possibility/ability (**podemos ir ao museu** – we can/could go to the museum).
Conheces algum sítio?	Do you know a place? **Conhecer** is used for 'to know' when we mean being acquainted with a person or a place.
Toca uma banda/um grupo	There's a band playing. Notice that in Portuguese the word order can differ greatly from the English equivalent, so here we're actually saying: 'Plays a band'. Or you could also say: **Há música ao vivo** (lit: There is music live). Don't worry about why this is; just try to learn expressions in Portuguese as they are.

Find expressions in the dialogue to convey the following: ⊙ 74-75

1. What do you want to do now?
2. We could have a drink.
3. Do you know a place?
4. There's a band playing.
5. Shall we go into this pub?
6. We're going to the bar.

· ·

Match the names of the drinks with the photos.

1. vinho do Porto
2. um gin-tónico
3. uma cerveja

a.

b.

c.

· ·

How would you say the following? Check your answers by listening ⊙ 76
to the audio track.

1. What do you want to drink? *(use the informal form)*
2. a glass of port
3. with a lot of ice

· ·

Listen to the voices and make sure you have understood what ⊙ 77
the people are saying. Here are some questions to guide you:

1. What does the first person want with his gin and tonic?
2. What drink does the second person order?
3. What is happening tonight, and at what time?

Match the suggestions on the left with the activities on the right:

1. Porque é que não ...?   tomar algo, Ana

2. Podemos ...   entramos neste bar

3. Queres ...?   a um pub

4. Vamos ...?   ir ao museu se quiseres

Pronunciation Tips

We have seen throughout the course that Portuguese uses a lot of symbols above or below a letter to change its pronunciation. Let's look at some of them again:

estação, pensão, João

We've already met the frequent nasal pronunciation in Portuguese in Unit 4. Here are some more words for you to practise pronouncing nasally all the vowels that have a ~ (tilde) over them. Pronounce **ão** like the 'ow' in English 'owl'. Then try this tricky one which has two nasal pronunciations in one word! – **amanhã** (tomorrow).

inglês, três, têm

Another frequent symbol is the (∧) circumflex. Whenever you see it above a vowel, it is pronounced closed (like 'e' in the first letter of English 'engineer') and again you emphasise the syllable on which the accent is written.

música, está, gin-tónico, sítio

You'll find plenty of acute accents (´) above vowels. Say the words out loud and always stress the part with an accent on it: **MÚ**-si-ca, e-**STÁ**, gin-**TÓ**-ni-co, **SÍ**-ti-o.

 ## Listen up 2

Later the same evening, Katie, Ben and António are having fun in the jazz bar. Listen out for more drinks, the possibility of a dance and arrangements for getting back to the hotel.

⊙ 7 8

cantora *f*/cantor *m* or o/a vocalista	Singer or vocalist – **vocalista** is both masculine and feminine, but we can hear who is referred to because of the article **o** *m* or **a** *f*.
canta	He/she sings – from **cantar**, 'to sing'. Make tenho sono and estou cansado.
bonita/o *f/m*	good-looking
amigo *m*/amiga *f*	Literally "friend", these two words are used colloquially in a way equating to the English 'mate' or 'man'.
Porque é que não peço mais bebidas?	Why don't I order more drinks? **Peço** is from **pedir** ('to order').
Querem tomar mais alguma coisa?	Do you fancy something else (to drink)?
Não quero mais nada	I don't want anything else.
dançar	to dance
não danço muito bem.	I'm not a very good dancer/I don't dance very well.
Não tem mal	It doesn't matter.
homem	Literally, 'man', but can be used to speak directly to someone, in expressions like **Anda, homem!** ('Come off it, man!').
Anda!	Come on!
Tenho calor *m*	I'm hot
casa *f* de banho *m*	Toilet – you may see or hear various terms for the restrooms in public buildings: **casa de banho, WC, Toilet**
Aqui tens a tua cerveja	Here's your beer.
miúda	girl
Tenho sono/Estou cansado/a *m/f*.	I'm sleepy/tired. **Tenho sono** refers to feeling sleepy whereas **estou cansado/a** is used more for bodily weariness.
Chamamos um táxi?	Shall we call a taxi?
voltar	to return/go back
Estamos a cinco minutos a pé	It's five minutes on foot
Até amanhã	See you tomorrow!

| Querem tomar ...? | Lit. 'Do you want to take (consume) ...?' We can always use the structure **Quero/Queremos/Querem** + *infinitive of a verb* to express 'I want/we want/they want to ...' (e.g. to drink/eat). |
| tenho calor/sono | 'I'm hot/sleepy.' A number of expressions that would start with 'I am' in English begin with **tenho** ('I have') in Portuguese. Here we're actually saying 'I have heat' rather than 'I'm hot'. Here's a short list of similar expressions: |

tenho calor – I'm hot
tenho frio – I'm cold
tenho fome – I'm hungry
tenho sede – I'm thirsty
tenho sono – I'm sleepy
tenho sorte – I'm lucky

| Chamamos um táxi. | 'Let's call a taxi'/'Shall we call a taxi?' It's reassuring to see that there's absolutely no spelling change involved in turning a statement into a question – just add the question mark. |
| Chamamos um táxi? | |

Here are some anagrams of several words and expressions used in the dialogue. Can you solve them?

1. relonhcoat ....
2. natcrao ....
3. çnadar ....
4. sabbied ....
5. codansa ....

· ·

Can you say the following in Portuguese? Check your answers by listening to the audio track. 79

1. I don't dance very well.
2. I'm going to the toilet.
3. I'm sleepy.
4. Shall we call a taxi?

Make sure you've understood what is being said. Answer the ⊙ 80
following questions as you listen to the people talking:

1. What is said about the group's singer? ....
2. What solution is suggested to relieve the heat? ....
3. How far away is the hotel? ....
4. When will they next see each other? ....

••

Look at the questions on the left and fill in the answers on
the right.

This may seem a bit repetitive but you're practising changing the endings of the
verb forms. The first row has been completed to start you off:

Queres uma cerveja?   Sim, **quero** uma cerveja.

Danças bem?   Sim, ... bem.

Tens calor?   Sim, ... calor.

Estás cansado?   Sim, ... cansado.

Vais ao bar?   Sim, ... ao bar.

 ## Let's recap

In this unit we've looked at various ways of making suggestions. Here are
some model sentences to help you remember:

Vamos a um pub?

Porque é que não vamos a um pub?

Podemos ir a um pub?

Queres ir a um pub?

We also learned some useful new expressions with **ter**.

••

Now see how good your memory is. Below are some English expressions –
give the Portuguese for each, but in the negative form:

e.g. I'm not sleepy   **não** tenho sono

1. I'm from Lisbon.
2. I want a glass of port.

3. I'm thirty years old.

4. I'm going to the WC.

••

Choose the correct option to complete each sentence:

1. .... ir tomar algo.

   a. Vamos   **b.** Podemos   **c.** Tu   **d.** Estou

2. Porque é .... não pedimos mais bebidas?

   a. tenho   **b.** que   **c.** para   **d.** cerveja

3. Esta noite .... uma banda.

   a. jazz   **b.** estás   **c.** doce   **d.** toca

4. .... chamar um táxi.

   a. Tu   **b.** Há   **c.** Vamos   **d.** Tens

Mantendo contacto
Keeping in touch

12

We'll consolidate what we've learned so far in the course, as well as looking ahead to meeting up with our new Portuguese friends in the future. To do this, we'll be having a look at the language of communication – phones, mobiles, texting and email.

Traveller's tip

It's great to make friends in Portugal during your visit, and to keep in touch once you're back in your own country. It's an ideal way to practise the language, as well as giving you a social platform for future visits.

These days, your mobile phone – **o telemóvel** - and email – **o correio eletrónico/o email** - are the two most common tools for keeping in touch. In fact, you may already have used email in Portugal – in **um cibercafé** (internet café) – and may be used to phoning or texting home by mobile.

You'll see that the Portuguese are every bit as technologically savvy as foreign visitors are, and that there are a range of telephony companies working in tandem with your mobile service provider back home. Don't be surprised if, when you switch on your mobile on emerging from the airport in Portugal, your screen lights up with the name of a local telephone network such as TMN, Vodafone or Optimus.

Roaming rates have dropped spectacularly over the last couple of years, but if you want to contact friends and family living in Portugal while you're there on holiday, you also have the option of buying a Portuguese SIM card or even a cheap mobile. You can also use the public phones on the streets for cheap national calls.

Cibercafés can be found in most Portuguese towns and cities, and rates tend to be very reasonable. You may even find your hotel has internet facilities available to guests.

In this unit we'll be revising questions and answers in the context of making plans for the future, using the language of communication.

Envias-me um email?	Will you send me an email?
Envio-te um sms.	I'll send you a text.
Qual é o teu número de telefone?	What's your phone number?

We'll also have a look at the two tricky words **por** and **para**.

 ## Listen up 1

Katie and Ben have reached the end of their holiday, and are swapping contact details with their new friend António. Listen out for two phone numbers and an email address.

 81

The trio have a farewell drink together before Katie and Ben leave for the airport. You'll hear departure and arrival times for the flight and a decision on how to get to the airport. ⊙ 82

Words and phrases 1

Qual é o teu número de telefone *m*?	What's your phone number?
Eu escrevo-te.	I'll write it down for you.
tens que marcar	you have to dial (from **ter que** – to have to)
o indicativo *m* da cidade *f*	the regional code (lit: the prefix of the city)
o meu número *m* de telemóvel *m*	my mobile number
Tens telemóvel?	Do you have a mobile phone?

dou-te	I'll give you (from **dar** – to give)
o meu endereço *m* de correio *m* eletrónico	my email address
Que tal irmos ir beber a última?	How about we go and have one last drink? **ir beber a última** to have one (drink) for the road
um pires de caracóis *m pl*	a saucer of snails
é para já	right away
A que horas sai o avião?	What time does your plane leave?
Podemos apanhar um táxi	We can get a taxi
Vamos de autocarro	We'll go/we're going by bus
É mais barato.	It's cheaper (lit: it's more cheap).
Acompanho-vos	I'll come with you (lit: I'll accompany you)
de qualquer forma	anyway

Unlocking the language 1

Qual é o teu número de telefone?

'What (lit. which) is your phone number?' Notice the word order – your number of telephone.

É o dois, um-três, quatro, oito-zero, seis, nove-um.

'It's 213480691.' To quote the phone number you begin with 'it's': **é o.** Then you state the digits either individually or in pairs – forty-eight, ninety-one, etc. But it's more common to state them individually, pause after the regional code and then pause after each pair. You can also pause after every three digits because all numbers are nine digits long.

o indicativo

'the code'. To ring Portugal from abroad you'll need the international code from your own country, then 351 (**três, cinco, um**) for Portugal, followed by the province-specific code – this is 21 (**vinte e um**) for Lisboa, 2 (**dois**) for Porto, and so on. Then you continue with the person's number.

o correio eletrónico

'electronic mail'. Increasingly, the Portuguese are using the English 'email'.

Ben.thompson44@
myemail.co.uk

The convention for pronouncing an email address is: Ben-**ponto**-thompson-quarenta-e-quatro-**arroba**-myemail-**ponto**-co-**ponto**-uk. The key words here are **ponto** for 'dot' and **arroba**, meaning 'at'. If there's no dot and you want to say 'all one word', use **tudo junto**. If there's a hyphen (-) just say **hífen**, and an underscore is either **traço inferior** or **traço baixo**.

acompanho-vos

'I'll accompany you'. The **–vos** is something similar to what we saw in Unit 9 (**vou-te**). It means 'you' and refers to two or more people (in this case, Ben and Katie). For clarity, compare the following, both spoken by António:

Acompanho-te, Katie (*informal, singular*)
Acompanho-vos, Katie e Ben (*plural*)

 Your turn 1

Find expressions in the dialogue to convey the following: 81–82

1. What's your phone number?
2. I'll write it down for you.
3. Have you got a mobile?
4. I'll give you my email address.
5. I'll come with you to the airport.
6. We can take a taxi.

Pronunciation Tip

mensagem, viagem
chega, português, obrigado

The **g** in Portuguese is pronounced like the 's' in English 'leisure' when it is followed by an 'e' or 'i' (**ge, gi**). However, when followed by a 'ue' or 'ui' (**gue, gui**), 'a' or 'o' (**ga, go**), it is pronounced like the 'g' in English 'good'. Try to practise: *por-tu-**GUÊS***.

· ·

How would you say the following? We've given you two to 83
get started. Check your answers by listening to the audio track.

O meu número de telemóvel é o …

1. 213456702 – dois, um, três, quatro, cinco, seis, sete, zero, dois
2. 228456702 – dois, dois, oito, quatro, cinco, seis, sete, zero, dois
3. 243550794
4. 262271360
5. 254316298

Two Portuguese friends have given you their email addresses, 84
but some of the letters are missing. Try to write down the missing
letters as you hear them.

Dou-te o meu endereço de correio eletrónico:

1. te_ _ sa-l_ _bo_ @ y _ h_ _.p _
2. n _ n_ .go _ _ s @c_ _ x._ t

. . . .

Match the questions or suggestions on the left with the English
translations on the right.

1.	Dá-me ...?	Have you got ...?
2.	Tens ...?	What's ...?
3.	Qual é ...?	We could ...
4.	Escreves-me ...?	Will you give me ...?
5.	Podemos ...	Will you write it down for me ...?

 Listen up 2

Katie and Ben have reached the airport. Now it's time to say 85
goodbye to António. Listen out for more contact details, as well as
various ways of saying goodbye.

Words and phrases 2

Envias-me um sms (uma mensagem curta)?	Will you send me a text? Usually you will hear either **sms** or **mensagem curta** ('short message'). **Enviar** is 'to send'.
de Londres	from London
com certeza	of course
Mas não tenho o teu número!	But I don't have your number!
Já o/a tenho.	I've got it now.
tens o meu endereço de correio eletrónico?	Do you have my email address?
não o tenho	I don't have it
A sério! Não to dei?	What a disaster! (lit: Really? I didn't give it to you?)
Amanhã envio-te as fotos	Tomorrow I'll send you the photos – notice the spelling of **f-** not **ph-**
Dá-me dois beijos.	Give me two kisses – the standard greeting or farewell gesture (one kiss on each cheek).
Obrigada/o por tudo.	Thanks for everything.
Toma conta de ti!	Look after yourself/Take care.
Até pró ano que vem.	See you next year (lit: until the year that comes). This is the colloquial version; the formal expression is **Até para o ano que vem.**
Vou-vos visitar	I'm going to visit you
Até breve.	See you soon (lit: until soon).
Boa viagem.	Safe journey/Have a good trip.

Unlocking the language 2

Temos que apanhar	'We have to catch' – remember that when a part of **ter** is followed by **que**, it means 'must' or 'have to'.
Envias-me ...? Envio-te ...	Notice that Portuguese can imply an action in the future even when we're using the simple present tense. What the Portuguese is literally saying is 'You send me ...?'/'I send you ...'. But in English a future tense works better: 'Will you send me ...?'/'I'll send you ...'.

| Por *or* para? | Both these words can mean 'for', and they can cause confusion for students of Portuguese. There isn't space here to go into detail, but as a simple rule, use **para** when you're talking about the purpose or intended use or destination of something (**o comboio para Lisboa**) and **por** if you mean 'because of', 'on account of', etc. (**Obrigada por tudo.**). |
| Até ... | Literally meaning 'until', this is very useful when you want to say 'see you (at some point in the future)': **Até amanhã!** ('See you tomorrow'), **Até breve!** ('See you soon'), **Até pró ano que vem!** ('See you next year'). |

⌐ Your turn 2

Can you remember the expressions needed to construct this short dialogue in Portuguese? Refer to the dialogue above if you need to.   85

1. Have you got my email address?

2. Yes, I've got it.

3. I'll send you the photos tomorrow.

4. Thanks for everything.

5. See you soon.

6. Have a good trip.

••

Can you say the following in Portuguese? They're all fragments of language to do with communication. Check your answers by listening to the audio track. 86

1. I haven't got a mobile.

2. It's (*when introducing your phone number*)

3. the area code

4. 'dot' (*in an email address*)

5. 'at' (*in an email address*)

...sten to one person giving an email address, and another giving a phone number. Try to write them both down as you listen:

1. ....

2. ....

•••

Write out the phone numbers in full. We've given you one to get you started.

218231697	dois um oito-dois três um-seis nove sete
227247642	....
219183240	....
205670306	....
263418299	....

Let's recap

In this unit we've looked at various structures to do with exchanging contact information. Here are some model sentences:

O meu número de telefone é o dois, um, quatro – dois, dois, seis – sete, zero, oito. (214226708)

O endereço do meu correio eletrónico é: teresa-ponto-santos-arroba-netcabo-ponto-pt (teresa.santos@netcabo.pt)

•••

Now see how good your memory is. Can you remember how to say these?

1. Have you got my address?

2. I've goit.

3. Two ways of saying 'I'll send you a text'.

Choose the correct option to complete each sentence:

1. Obrigada .... tudo.

   a. de   **b.** para   **c.** por   **d.** em

2. Até pró .... que vem.

   a. amanhã   **b.** ano   **c.** visita   **d.** hora

3. ....-vos visitar.

   a. Queremos   **b.** Prefiro   **c.** Tenho   **d.** Vou

4. .... viagem.

   a. Bom   **b.** Boa   **c.** Bem   **d.** Bons

Revisão 2
Revision 2

Age

Remember that in Portuguese we 'have' an age, rather than 'being' it. Make sure you can say your age using **tenho ... anos.**

Listen up

Listen to the people talking about their ages and write down how old each person is:

⦿ 88

1. Raquel ....
2. Paulo ....
3. Teresa ....
4. Bernardo ....

Spelling

Refer to the alphabet in Unit 3, and practise spelling out your name and address. It's a good idea to keep coming back to this, and to take as many opportunities as possible to spell words out.

Tu and você

Your use of the informal and polite versions of Portuguese verbs will depend very much on what sort of people you're mixing with, and the formality of the situations you experience. It's a good idea to take some time out and look through all the dialogues we've covered, practising converting polite verbs to informal, and vice versa. Remember that in most cases, the informal variant will have an '**-s**' or '**-es**' on the end (e.g. **queres** – versus the polite **quer**).

For a bit of practice, try changing the following polite forms into informal versions. The first one is done for you:

Polite	Informal
Quer uma cerveja?	Queres uma cerveja?
Você é canadiano?	....
Vai a Lisboa?	....
Tem sono?	....
Fala português?	....

Want to/have to/am going to

Have a look over these structures, and set up a stock of things you can talk about that you want to do (**quero visitar o Museu de Arte Moderna**), have to do (**tenho que estudar**) and are going to do (**vou tomar um café**).

If you're into culture and leisure activities and want to learn more about what Portugal has to offer in your field of interest, the internet is a great source of information. You can start by doing a search for your favourite activity/sport, including key words like 'Portugal' in the search. Many official and informal Portuguese websites (the internet country code for Portugal is .pt) have little flags where you can click to read the information in a number of languages: why not click the English text to read what you want to know, then try reading the Portuguese version to see how much you understand. You can print off key pages and look at the two versions side by side, using a dictionary to highlight useful vocabulary. It's a great way of building up your vocabulary and your confidence in areas of interest. If you like sport, you can try searching terms like "Federação Portuguesa de (+ name of sport taken from dictionary)" to access a wealth of information. (When you type a search term, you can have small letters for any capitals and you don't need to have any accents on letters.) Similarly, if you like theatre, cinema, ballet, museums, etc., you can take key words from the dictionary and type them into a search engine. Once you get bitten by the Portuguese bug, there will be no stopping you!

Shopping

You've seen that there are a lot of conventions in the language of shopping. Have a look back through the dialogues, and try substituting the items bought for items you'd be likely to buy in Portugal. Make a vocabulary list to increase your confidence.

Speak out

Can you remember how you'd say the following? Try saying the sentences out loud.   ⊙ 89

1. I'm looking for a white shirt. ....

2. How much is it? ....

3. It's a bit small. ....

4. I'll take it, thanks. ....

Likes and dislikes

Starting with the simple formula of **gosto de ...** or **não gosto de ...**, you can very easily cover your likes and dislikes. Remember that you don't have to limit this to items or concepts (**gosto de café, gosto de arte**); you can talk about activities too (**gosto de estudar**). Asking others about their preferences is easy too: there's the informal **Gostas?** or the polite **Gosta ...?**

Listen up 2

Listen to people talking about their likes and dislikes, and answer the questions below: ⊙ 90

1. Joana likes port – true or false?

2. Who likes football?

3. José likes Lisboa very much – true or false?

4. To what extent does Marisa like working?

Out and about

If your interests coincide with some of the scenarios we've set up on this course – museums, eating out, a football match, shopping – then you've got a good linguistic platform on which to build. But don't forget that all the structures will be transferable to other situations, and with a bit of dictionary work to get hold of the specific vocabulary for your preferred activity, you'll be able to work out dialogues of your own.

If you can, of course, you should also talk to Portuguese people in order not to lose contact with the language.

Communication

Write down all your contact details, then think about pronouncing everything in Portuguese. It's a good idea to write it all out longhand – e.g. if your phone number begins 218 then write down **'dois, um, oito'**. This is especially important for your email address: remember the magic words **ponto** for 'dot' and **arroba** for '@'. Keep practising these until you find you can say them all fluently without referring to your paper, and don't forget the expressions for texting.

Boa sorte!

Good luck!

HAVE YOU SEEN OUR FULL PORTUGUESE RANGE? PICK A TITLE TO FIT YOUR LEARNING STYLE.

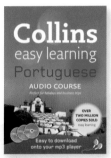

Audio Course
£14.99

Collins Easy Learning Audio Courses

This exciting course allows learners to absorb the basics at home or on the move, without the need for thick textbooks or complex grammar.

Collins Phrasebooks

These portable, easy-to-use phrasebooks will ensure you get the right word – every time.

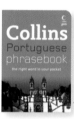

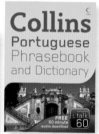

Gem Phrasebook
£4.50

Phrasebook and Dictionary
£4.99

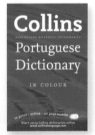

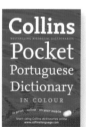

Dictionary
£15.99

Pocket Dictionary
£9.99

Gem Greek Dictionary
£5.99

Collins Dictionaries

Our bestselling dictionaries help you take you learning to the next level.

Collins